TEACHING
P.R.A.Y.E.R.

TEACHING
P.R.A.Y.E.R.

Guidance for
Pastors and Church Leaders

BRANT D. BAKER

ABINGDON PRESS / Nashville

TEACHING P.R.A.Y.E.R.:
GUIDANCE FOR PASTORS AND CHURCH LEADERS

This book is printed on acid-free paper.

Library of Congress Cataloging-in-Publication Data

Baker, Brant D., 1958-
    Teaching P.R.A.Y.E.R. : guidance for pastors and church leaders / Brant D. Baker.
        p. cm.
    ISBN 0-687-04864-8 (alk. paper)
    1. Prayer. I. Title: Teaching prayer. II. Title.

BV210.2 .B275 2001
248.3'2—dc21

2001022582

01 02 03 04 05 06 07 08 09 10—10 9 8 7 6 5 4 3 2 1

MANUFACTURED IN THE UNITED STATES OF AMERICA

To
Sadie Twilley,
one of God's great prayer saints

CONTENTS

Introduction

Relational Speech

How can we pray? How in the world is it possible to adequately address the supreme God of all creation? If we get nervous thinking about an audience with a king, a president, a judge, or even a school principal, how in the world are we to have an audience with Almighty God? How can we pray?

Yet how can we *not* pray? If our very life is drawn from our relationship with God, if our hope for eternal life is rooted and grounded in Jesus Christ, if our hope for abundant life depends on our openness to the Spirit's leading, then how can we do anything but pray? Descartes said, "I think, therefore I am." He had it almost right: we say, "I pray, therefore I am."

And into this tension of not knowing how to pray, but knowing we must pray if we are to live, comes a further challenge: How can we learn to pray? The sad truth is that prayer is a skill more likely to be learned from the local chapter of Toastmasters than in church, insofar as prayer, commonly conceived and practiced, involves a facility in public speaking more than a facility in conversation with Almighty God.

Let us begin with a definition of prayer as "relationship-specific" or "specialized" communication. I have many relationships in my life. One of these is with my wife. I have one way of talking to my wife that is different from the way I talk to other people. In talking to my wife I know, among other things, that for her "anything unexpected is probably bad." Thus, I carefully introduce my latest wild idea with phrases such as "You probably won't like this right away" or "I'd like you to think about this before you react." After our many years together, she understands this code and is able to hear what I'm saying with at least some assurance that I recognize I'm sharing a wild idea.

I have another way of talking to my golf buddies. We speak a "specialized" language that revolves around our common passion.

9

If I ask one of them for a read on my putt, he's likely to say, "I see about a cup of left to right break," and I know exactly what he means. We use some specialized and some everyday vocabulary, and mix into that words and phrases based on our past experiences together, so that our conversation would be somewhat challenging for an outsider to decipher.

So too there is a kind of speech for our life with God. It is relationship-specific in that we know certain things about God, and God knows us: our time together, be it long or short, has taught us a few things about each other. It is specialized in that we use certain "insider" language, words and concepts such as *confession, petition, supplication, grace, mercy,* and even *pleading the blood.*

The idea that prayer is a relationship-specific and a specialized kind of communication fits with most people's twofold understanding of prayer. On the one hand, we understand that prayer is simply talking to God. On the other hand, we fear that God doesn't seem to hear because we don't quite know the "insider" language of this particular relationship.

All of this points to the need to expand our understanding of prayer. The material in the following pages suggests that there is only a small amount of "insider" language, and that prayer is best defined as *relationship.* Learning to communicate in this relationship, as in any other, is then a matter of time and practice.

ACTS versus PRAYER

As a beginning, let's talk about ACTS. Many people first learned to pray with this helpful acronym, which outlines four movements of prayer: Adoration, Confession, Thanksgiving, and Supplication. This is a valid approach to prayer. It recognizes that prayer is more than "asking for things," including as it does time for adoring and thanking God.

The ACTS approach, however, is missing at least two important elements. First, it is without connection to the great prayer book of the Bible, the Psalms. Starting our prayer with a psalm helps ensure a foundation for what follows and helps provide us with a language for our conversation with God. Second, the ACTS approach has no clear time for listening. If prayer is essentially a relationship, and if communication in a healthy relationship is a dialogue, where do we stop talking and listen to God in our prayer? One could even argue that, in a relationship as unequal as ours with God, it might make sense to let *God* do most of the talking!

Dissatisfaction with the absence of the psalms and of a time for listening has given rise to an alternative acronym—PRAYER. In this outline there are six movements in prayer:

- *Psalming* (starting prayer with a selection from *The Book of Prayers*);

- *Reconciling* (confession and forgiveness);

- *Adoring* (including thanksgiving and praise);

- *Yielding* (listening);

- *Entreating* (intercession and petition—the "asking" part of prayer); and

- *Realizing* (living the spiritual life or, as it is sometimes called, "practicing the presence").

What's Ahead

The first chapter, "Prayer in the Postmodern Era," is an introduction to our topic and presents the challenge of teaching on it. There is a brief overview of the current cultural-religious climate, addressing the vestiges of an Enlightenment culture that is suspicious of spiritual reality, as well as of the emerging postmodern culture that shows a deep hunger for spiritual things. The first class is a typical "getting started" session that includes the obvious group-building needs, covenanting issues, concerns listing and questions, basic definitions of prayer, and an introduction to the PRAYER acronym.

The second chapter, "The Lord's Prayer as Pattern," looks at the Lord's Prayer. The class session offers an overview of the Lord's Prayer, with the suggestion that Jesus intended this prayer to be used as a pattern or outline for our own prayers, not as something we offer by rote. A handout explores several ways of naming the parts of the prayer, and the six moves of the current prayer study are correlated to the six petitions of the prayer that Jesus taught. Chapter 3, on "Psalming," looks at the place of the psalms in the life of prayer. An overview of the various types of psalms is presented to the class and helps set the stage for a class discussion about the orality of the psalms in their original usage. The class session explores reasons for praying out loud and then works to get people started praying the psalms.

Chapter 4, on "Reconciling," focuses on confession and forgiveness as central acts of prayer in the Judeo-Christian tradition. The chapter examines not only the theologic but also the therapeutic centrality of reconciliation, especially as brought forth in Jesus' life and teaching. The class session utilizes an "old-fashioned Bible study" to lay the foundation for understanding the central role of reconciliation in prayer, and it includes a visualization exercise that leads participants to encounter the power of this concept through a meeting with Jesus around one of the Gospel stories.

The fifth chapter, "Adoring," overviews work in the area of prayer, personality, and spiritual types. The purpose of this overview is to give participants a sense of freedom regarding prayer styles. The class session emphasizes that prayers of adoration and thanksgiving can take a variety of forms: not only speech and writing, but also music, art, or dance.

Chapter 6, "Yielding," underscores the importance of prayer as a dialogical activity that includes silence and listening. The chapter explores the question of discernment, suggests that we often hear God's "ideational voice," and offers ways to test what we think we hear. After covering this material, the class session also offers ten to twenty minutes of silence in which to listen.

Chapter 7, "Entreating," seeks to develop a theology of intercessory prayer, especially on the question of unanswered prayer. A catechetical-style handout attempts to deal with some of the basic questions that tend to be barriers to prayer.

The last chapter, "Realizing," offers some reflections on what the spiritual life might look like in today's world. Can we join Brother Lawrence and "practice the presence"? What changes can and should we expect from being people of prayer? How can church leaders help others to grow in grace, sanctification, and spirituality? The class session includes a time to brainstorm ways for realizing God's presence day by day, moment by moment.

Nuts, Bolts, and Prayer

As you prepare to teach this class, you will want to consider several things, such as time and place for the class, food and childcare arrangements, and the way to handle publicity and promotion. But before any of that, and throughout all of it, don't forget to pray!

How typical it would be for me to go about planning an entire class on prayer without once actually praying for the class. It is a strange reality of practicing our faith that we can go about doing spiritual things without actually doing anything spiritual.

Utilizing the PRAYER acronym to shape praying for this class might mean *Psalming* the prayers of the community (using, for example, Psalm 84, 133, 149, or 150). The last of these might lead naturally to a time of *Adoring* and praise for what God is doing in the life of the church and its people as plans for this prayer study are under way. (A note here, to be repeated throughout, is that the moves of prayer are not necessarily linear. If a psalm leads to *Adoring* as the second move of prayer rather than *Reconciling* because it's the next on the list, then we should feel free to follow that direction in our praying.) Prayers (and acts) of *Reconciling* could be offered for relationships in the teacher's own life, and for those individuals brought together for this class who might otherwise remain apart. A long and intentional period of *Yielding* would go far in answering many of the remaining nuts-and-bolts questions as we seek God's best intention for as little a thing as what classroom to use. *Entreating* would give voice to all the needs and concerns surrounding the class and speak into reality God's will concerning them. *Realizing*, as enacted prayer, would carry out the plans for the class with a growing awareness of God as partner in the whole endeavor.

Time and Place

No doubt there are some existing forums in the life of the church in which this class could be taught: Sunday school, a youth or adult Bible study group, a women's or men's prayer group, or even a retreat. Another option would be to offer the class as a special opportunity outside of these usual forums, one evening a week or even on a Saturday morning. Many people are willing to make short-term commitments for a study of interest such as this.

Whatever the case, be sure to discuss your plan with the necessary church leaders (committee, board, etc.) to get input and gain a broad base of support.

The most likely place for the group to meet is a classroom (or possibly a home), but you may want to give consideration to the sanctuary, at least for the closing prayer. Each of the lessons includes a closing prayer or a hands-on time to practice what has been proposed in the lesson. Classroom settings are great for teaching and conversations, but moving to another setting may help connect the intellectual aspect of the class with the spiritual practice of what has been discussed. If a move to the sanctuary isn't possible, consider setting up another classroom as a prayer chapel. Indirect lighting, comfortable seating options (including floor pillows for sitting or kneeling), soft music (probably instrumental) or even a small fountain, and selected points of visual interest (a painting or scripture) would set a more worshipful tone.

Food and Childcare

Depending on when and where you meet, food and childcare may be issues to consider. After years of a morning quiet time, a cup of coffee has become an important tactile part of my spiritual life. If you choose to serve food as well as beverages, be sure to offer an alternative to sweets such as fresh fruit or crackers.

Childcare is important only if you want to attract younger people to the group. Even if there is only one person who will use these arrangements, having made them is worth the extra effort. The likelihood is that one young couple or single parent will quickly invite a friend who also has children, and your group will grow. Providing childcare will also allow you to expand your publicity efforts.

Publicity and Promotion

Your church likely has a number of in-house communications vehicles. Newsletters, Sunday bulletins, and announcements from the pulpit are all part of the intricate web of redundant communication. Marketing experts suggest that it takes a minimum of seven exposures before people begin to consider the product in question. Start your publicity at least a month in advance to give people time to clear their calendars. Create posters, make announcements from the pulpit, or perhaps do a series of brief skits (that illustrate, for example, our usual challenges and frustrations about praying "correctly," unanswered prayer, and fear of praying out loud), concluding each with an invitation to come to the class.

A more aggressive publicity campaign might include placing an advertisement in the local paper, putting up posters in the grocery story or library, or sending a mailer to people in your church's neighborhood. (This is where having the childcare issue covered can open doors.) Since a study on the basics of prayer might attract a lot of seekers, you might want to think again about the time and place questions: Is the class to be offered at a time that conveniences a church population, or at a time that will attract unchurched folk from the neighborhood?

Getting Ready to Teach

Teaching P.R.A.Y.E.R. is designed as a quick and easy resource for pastors and teachers. It should take about an hour to read each chapter, make copies of the class handouts, and pull together any other resources you might need. The class handouts can be found at the end of each chapter and may be reproduced in sufficient numbers for the class. Each chapter ends with a section called "Teaching the Class," a step-by-step guide for each week's lesson that will tell you when and how to use these handouts. You might consider making the copies on different color paper from week to week, three-hole punching them, and providing participants with an inexpensive notebook in which to keep them.

Additional preparation time should be allowed for chapter 5, which calls for having an assortment of arts and crafts materials on hand, and these may take a little more time to gather from the Sunday school supply closet. This chapter will also be strengthened if leaders will take the time to provide participants with a personality test. The Kiersey Temperament Sorter can be found in *Please Understand Me* by David Kiersey and Marilyn Bates. The test can also be purchased separately.[1] The leader is instructed to distribute these as part of the "At Home This Week" assignment in chapter 4.

There Are No Experts

You are planning to teach others to pray. This is a daunting task for even the strongest ego. Here are a few words of hope (I hope!). First, there are no experts. Or perhaps we should say that all of us can be experts. In other words, if prayer is about a relationship, then we can always learn more about that relationship, but at the same time, presumably no one can know more about our relationship than we who are in it! In any case, we will get a lot farther if we present ourselves not as experts, but as humble co-learners on the journey together.

Second, although religion, faith, prayer, and the spiritual life are *personal*, they are not *private*. The great myth of our contemporary culture is that a relationship with God is a private relationship, and so no one can say anything to anyone about it. Christians have double trouble with this argument, both as people who are part of the prevailing culture and as people who remember Jesus' admonition that whenever we pray, we should go into our room, shut the door, and pray to our Father who is in secret (Matt. 6:6). As in some of the other cases he addresses in the Sermon on the Mount (almsgiving and fasting), Jesus is working to correct ostentatious behavior. There is a time for prayer in secret, and there is a time (as evidenced by Jesus' own practice) for prayer in public; there is a time for quiet worship in one's room, and a time (as evidenced by Jesus) for worship with the people of God. Andrew Murray suggests that balance between personal and corporate prayer is like a tree: "For its full development, a tree has its root hidden in the ground and its stem growing up into the sunlight. In the same way prayer equally needs both the hidden secrecy in which the soul meets God alone and the public fellowship with those who find in the name of Jesus their common meeting place" (86). To say prayer is a private matter is most likely an excuse offered by cautious secular people when faced by zealous Christians.

Finally, don't forget that the first step is to "pray-tice what you preach!" Pray prayers of thanksgiving that you have been called to teach. Pray prayers of entreaty for yourself and those who will learn with you. Pray prayers of yielding that you may hear what God would have you say and do.

Chapter One

Prayer in the Postmodern Era

How can we pray—and yet how can we *not* pray—in times like these? The questions posed in the introduction take on added poignancy when framed by cultural considerations. It is one thing to ask questions of prayer in a "pure" spiritual environment, where a certain measure of friendly faith can be presupposed. It is another thing altogether to pose such questions amidst the often hostile clamor of culture.

There is a danger in trying to address too specifically the current cultural climate. Culture, by its very nature, is constantly reinventing itself. But whether it is faddism or millennialism or postmodernism, a substantive shift is in the air. The long reign of modernity, which was crowned in the Enlightenment, is coming to an end. Rigid rationalism, unbending linear thinking, and isolating specialization are giving way to heightened metaphysical awareness, integrative reasoning, and interdisciplinary relationships.

What is the place of prayer in the midst of these changes? In a sense it would appear to be a place poised calmly between the fading modernism and the emerging postmodernism. Another way of saying this is that prayer is not threatened by the two questions posed earlier, questions that are representative of these respective ages. "How can we pray?" is the fair question of modernism, pointing to the psychological and scientific concerns that the Enlightenment brought to bear on the practice of prayer. "How can we not pray?" is the hopeful question of postmodernism, pointing to a sense of connection with the wonder around us. Let's look at each of these in turn.

"How Can We Pray?"
Prayer and the Enlightenment

As far back as the 1930s, Friedrich Heiler gave voice to the particular questions that an Enlightenment viewpoint raised for prayer. In his comprehensive historical and psychological study, Heiler noted that prayer had devolved from "living intercourse" with God into mere monologue. Modernity had followed the lead of Freud and Kant, who understood prayer as self-deception and soliloquy.[1] Heirs of this view, even those who faithfully sought to pray, were more than likely simply meditating on the qualities and nature of God (100). Heiler was particularly despairing of formal, liturgical, written prayers, which are "but a faint reflection of the burning prayer of the heart" (xix).

Some decades later, Jacques Ellul took Heiler's assessment a step further, noting: "If prayer is not the deepest and the most completely free cry from the heart it seems to me to be indecent" (v-vi). Ellul suggested that primitive peoples were inspired to pray out of either fear or need. We who are well-defended and provisioned, therefore, have less motivation. Furthermore, the wonder of nature, which was once a source of inspiration to pray, is effaced and desacralized by science and technology (37-40).

The legacy of the Enlightenment leaves us with essentially four kinds of questions related to prayer.[2]

- How can we pray if God is going to act anyway? (Superheated Calvinism)
- How can we pray if we're going to have to take action ourselves? (Lone-Rangerism)
- How can we pray if the answer is going to be vague? (The Ambiguity Syndrome)
- How can we pray if God isn't going to hear our prayer? (Lamentation Is Always an Option)

Let's address each of these questions in turn.

How can we pray if God is going to act anyway?
(Superheated Calvinism)

According to the understanding of some—or perhaps I should say, according to the fears of some—God is all-knowing, all-powerful, and sovereign. This being the case, why bother to pray? If God knows what needs to be done, has the power to do it, and is going to do it all anyway, why bother to pray?

I have teasingly called these kinds of thoughts "superheated Calvinism" after John Calvin, the father of such a strong view of God's sovereignty that it eventually gave rise to predestination. But Calvin himself would have rejected such a perverse notion of God's sovereignty. Calvin chides:

> But, someone will say, does God not know, even without being reminded, both in what respect we are troubled and what is expedient for us, so that it may seem in a sense superfluous that he should be stirred up by our prayers—as if he were drowsily blinking or even sleeping until he is aroused by our voice? But they who thus reason do not observe to what end the Lord instructed his people to pray, for he ordained it not so much for his own sake as for ours. (851-52)

Calvin then goes on to suggest six reasons why, despite God's sovereignty, God has so ordained prayer for our sake:

1. So our hearts are filled and fired with love of God.
2. So that no desires and wishes enter our hearts that we are ashamed to bring to God.
3. So that we remember to give thanks for answers to prayer.
4. So that, having received our desire and given thanks for it, we further meditate on God's kindness.
5. So that we value more greatly those things that have come to us as a result of prayer.
6. So that we better understand that God's promise to help us is real, and not merely the "wet-nursing" of words (852).

In John 14:13 Jesus says, "I will do whatever you ask in my name, so that the Father may be glorified in the Son." How can we pray if God is going to act anyway? The answer is right here: "so that the Father may be glorified in the Son." While God often seems to enjoy working behind the scenes, it also seems to be the case that God's action in response to our asking makes it clear that God has answered our prayer.

How can we pray if we're going to have to take action ourselves?
(Lone-Rangerism)

In his wonderful book *Don't Just Stand There, Pray Something*, Ronald Dunn opens with a picture of prayer that is probably typical for many of us. In his mind's eye Dunn pictures a "little Spanish mission in the desert." In front there is a monk in traditional garb, his hands clasped "prayerfully" in front of him, looking monkish: timid, quiet, perhaps even a bit fragile. The monk is looking up at the Lone Ranger and Tonto. Their horses are "straining at the reins," nostrils flared, ready to charge off in a cloud of dust. The Lone Ranger and Tonto have their guns drawn, and "their faces are fixed in grim determination. The monk says something about going with them."

> "You are a brave man, Father," the masked man says, "but it may be dangerous. You had better stay here where it's safe."
> "But I want to help," the monk says.
> The strong yet kind eyes of the masked man fasten on the man of God. "You can pray."
> Suddenly the great white horse rears up on its hind legs, and with a wave of his hat and a hearty "Heigh Ho Silver—Awa-a-a-ay!" the Lone Ranger and his faithful companion gallop off to the danger that awaits them.

"The camera of my imagination," says Dunn, "does not follow the priest into the mission to watch him pray. It chases after the Lone Ranger and Tonto. That's where the action is" (15-16).

It is tempting to say, "Prayer and action go together." But even to phrase it this way buys into the Enlightenment view that prayer is not action, prayer is prayer. Yet anyone who has ever prayed in earnest and for an extended period knows how exhausting prayer can be. (One great prayer saint in a church I served, a woman in her eighties, can grip your hands and hold a posture for thirty minutes, by the end of which your muscles feel as if you've been to the gym. Talk about muscular Christianity!)

Jesus says, "Abide in me as I abide in you. Just as the branch cannot bear fruit by itself unless it abides in the vine, neither can you unless you abide in me. I am the vine, you are the branches. Those who abide in me and I in them bear much fruit, because *apart from me you can do nothing*" (John 15:4-5, emphasis added). Jacques Ellul suggests that even when we think we are "doing it ourselves" (because God hasn't answered), we are in fact doing it because we have been given the strength and ability to do whatever is needed— we have been given resources we didn't have until we prayed (127).

How can we pray when we're going to have to take action ourselves? How can we not!

How can we pray if the answer is going to be vague? *(The Ambiguity Syndrome)*

We might call this "Unanswered Prayer: Part 1." Some prayer appears to us painfully unanswered (see below). Other prayer seems answered—sort of. Maybe an event would have just happened anyway, or maybe it was just a coincidence: such is our inheritance from the Enlightenment.

The Christian response to the Ambiguity Syndrome has been *remembrance.* The biblical record is full of calls to remember, as the covenant is rehearsed again and again ("Hear, O Israel . . ."). In worship, this remembering is done sacramentally ("Do this in remembrance of me"). In Christian education, it is done through narrative as we tell both the biblical story and our own (testimony). In prayer, this remembering is done as we give thanks for what God has done (and here the practice of journaling can be an invaluable help).

In Mark 8 there is an unbelievable series of stories that illustrates the point. In the first story, Jesus feeds the four thousand (vv. 1-10). In the next segment, some Pharisees come and seek a sign from Jesus to test him. Now, admittedly, they come from a different region than the one in which the preceding miracle occurred, but it is still hard to conceive their demand. Getting back into the boat, Jesus begins talking about the Pharisees by using an image of leaven, and the disciples start to worry about not remembering bread. Jesus finally bursts out, "Why are you talking about having no bread? Do you still not perceive or understand? Are your hearts hardened? Do you have eyes, and fail to see? Do you have ears, and fail to hear? *And do you not remember?*" (Mark 8:17-18, emphasis added).

Most Christians probably live under the fantasy that, were they to witness all that Jesus said and did, they would be much more sensible than the disciples—sensible, in the sense of having eyes to see and ears to hear. But the truth is that those around Jesus were common sense, no-nonsense, dollars-and-cents kinds of people, but they still couldn't remember what Jesus had done just hours before. In other words, they were people perhaps a lot like us.

How can we pray if the answer is going to be vague? The truth is, we may just not be sensible enough to see, hear, and remember what really happened.

How can we pray if God isn't going to hear our prayer? (Lamentation Is Always an Option)

Here we get down to cases. The relentless eye of the Enlightenment has made it ever so clear that there are some times when the heavens are silent. This is, of course, not new information; the biblical record attests to this (especially the psalms). It's just that, in our information age, we have more evidence: for example, the stories of those who cried out to the Lord and still died in gas chambers and concentration camps.

In a poetry anthology entitled "Unanswered Prayers," the *Atlantic Monthly* (June 1997) presented some modern-day psalms of lament. One in particular spoke of the deep pain that unanswered prayer entails at the personal level. It was written by Patricia Hooper:

PRAYER

Lord, I call to you—
there is someone
I want you to follow home.
The night is cold.
The wet leaves hide the edges
of the dark path. He
is lost. I would
go with him if I could,
put my arms around him,
share my coat. He is
three hundred miles
away. No one else
sees him. Do you
see him, his step hurried
through the black rain?
Or are you
still busy, as you were when,
before he harmed himself
the last time, he was the one
who called? (97)

The poem gives poignant voice to human anger for unanswered prayer. Many children of the Enlightenment have found freedom and release in such angry speech toward God. But polite Christians cringe at such an emotion and would just as soon not put God on the spot. One result has been "safe" prayers: unspecific, weak, and anemic. In the larger culture the result has been a lack of prayer altogether. Many people think, *Why bother?*

Does God hear prayer? Jesus told an interesting parable in this regard. In Luke 11:5-8 we find the story of a friend who comes at midnight seeking a loaf of bread for unexpected company. The entreated neighbor responds, "Do not bother me; the door has already been locked, and my children are with me in bed; I cannot get up and give you anything."

Most interpreters of this story turn it into a parable of persistence, with the unfortunate result of suggesting that our prayers are sent to a sleepy, grumpy, grudging God who finally has to do something in order to get back to bed.

A better interpretation of the parable, however, is based on Middle Eastern understandings of hospitality. The sleepy neighbor finally gets up because he wants to preserve his honor by doing the right thing. The point of the parable is then made in the comparison: if your neighbor knows this much about honor, providing you with what you ask, how much more will God provide (and so v. 13: "If you then, who are evil, know how to give good gifts to your children, how much more will the heavenly Father give the Holy Spirit to those who ask him!") (Bailey, 119ff.).

Thus, our first response to the question of unanswered prayer is that prayer is always heard because God's honor is on the line. Put another way, God's nature is proved in hearing our prayers.

So if God does hear our prayers, what explains "unanswered" prayers? One Christian response is to note that prayers apparently answered "no" may actually be getting answered "not yet." Sometimes God answers later in order to answer better. A good biblical example is the story of Elizabeth and Zechariah. They had wanted a son, prayed for a son, and finally thought themselves too old to have a son. Then God gave them something better than a son. God gave them John the Baptist, a son who would be a great prophet and prepare the way for God's Messiah.

But having said all this, we finally get down to the fact that some prayers are unanswered. The heavenly "NO" rings undeniably in our ears when we've prayed for someone's recovery and the person still dies. There is little comfort in promises of eternity when the prayer was aimed at life today.

It is in these times, as we struggle between our emotions and our trust in God, that the church has turned to a special collection of prayers known as the *psalms of lament.* I will have more to say about these prayers in chapter 3, but for now suffice it to say that they give voice to all the anger, sorrow, pain, and hopelessness that is part of our shared life. It is significant that these prayers comprise nearly one-third of the psalms, as if to suggest that the Bible knows we will need an added measure of this kind of prayer language.

How can we pray if God isn't going to hear our prayer? First, by clinging to the primary affirmation that God wants better things for us than we want for ourselves. Ruth Graham, Billy Graham's wife, once said, "If God answered every prayer of mine, I would have married the wrong man seven times" (Dunn, 198). Second, by clinging to the biblical language of lament. In his pain-racked daze, Jesus on the cross reached for the language that was written on his heart and cried out from the psalms of lament, "My God, my God, why have you forsaken me?" Sometimes that's all that can be said, and it is fitting that it be said in the church among people of faith.

"How Can We Not Pray?" Prayer and Postmodernism

The questions about prayer posed by postmodernism are significantly different from those of the Enlightenment. Indeed, there is a two-sidedness in asking, "How can we not pray?" For in one sense it points to an openness and hunger in our society for the Other, but in another sense it points to a *wide*-openness and hunger in our society to virtually any Other.

Just what is postmodernism? The marks of postmodernism have been variously categorized as: being right-brained as well as left-brained and being intuitive as well as rational (Morgenthaler, 24); a shift from written to oral (what is written is no longer always reliable or the only source of knowledge); a shift from truth that is universal to truth that is particular (so that what is true may be true only in a particular place or situation, rather than truth—like scientific knowledge—being that which can be proved in every time and place); and a shift from truth that is timeless to truth that is timely (so that what is true today may not necessarily be what is true tomorrow—again, in contrast to how Enlightenment science construed truth) (Brueggemann 1993:6).

The shifts in perception and knowing have given rise to the "new science," which sees the world as much more interdependent and relational. There is also in the new science a kind of metaphysical awareness. While this awareness leads some thinkers to finally put God away altogether, others are led to ask, "How can we not pray?"

The shift in science may relate to a shift in worldview. "Worldview" is the collection of assumptions more or less given to a particular people in a particular time and place that in turn determines how they perceive and construe "reality" (and especially for our discussion, "spiritual reality"). In *The Powers That Be*, Walter Wink suggests that there are basically five worldviews, and that ours may be the first generation to have a conscious choice about which worldview we will believe in and live by (22).

According to Wink, the *ancient* worldview is the earliest and sees basically a two-part world of heaven and earth. What happens in one mirrors or affects what happens in the other. The next in line, the *spiritualist* worldview, has no dealings with earth, seeing it as an inferior or even unreal creation. Conversely, the *materialist* worldview denies the reality of heaven—matter is ultimate. This was the worldview of the Enlightenment. The *theological* worldview was a reaction to materialism, postulating a real heaven and a real earth, but suggesting that the two have little in common. The emerging paradigm is that of an *integral* worldview, which sees that everything has an inner and an outer reality. In this worldview, "Spirit is at the heart of everything, and all creatures are potential revealers of God" (15-20).

Each of these worldviews has its own idea of the use and efficacy of prayer. "Problems with prayer," says Wink, "are usually not a result of bad theology but of a wrong worldview" (182).

In the ancient worldview, where everything that happens on earth affects heaven and vice versa, prayer is "a matter of reversing the flow of fated events from on high to earth, and initiating a new flow from earth to heaven that causes God's will to be done 'on earth as it is in heaven.' The uninterrupted surge of consequences is dammed for a moment. Faith is tethered. New alternatives become feasible" (182-83).

In the spiritualist worldview, where matter is evil and creation a mistake or a hoax, prayer is a means of escaping the "error" of earth (183).

In the materialist worldview, that to which we have been heirs through the Enlightenment, there is no place for prayer. Wink suggests that our enslavement to a scientific model (in which there can be no physical effect without a physical cause) has impoverished our prayer (183). According to this worldview, prayer is superstition, and the best advice that can be given is to "get real."

In the theological worldview, an attempt was made to reclaim a place for prayer. But since science was handed the material world and religion was handed the spiritual world, there was an effective split between the two, and prayer was no better off than it was in the materialist worldview. The kindest thing that could be said for prayer in a theological worldview, says Wink, is that it was good for mental health; it was a time to examine one's conscience or to become centered (184).

But in the integral worldview, prayer is "absolutely central." "The spiritual is at the core of everything and is therefore infinitely permeable to prayer. In this view, the whole universe is a spirit-matter event, and the self is coextensive with the universe." In concert with the new science, Wink suggests that in such a world "we no longer know the limits of the possible. Therefore we pray for whatever we feel is right and leave the outcome to God. We live in expectation of miracles in a world reenchanted with wonder" (184).

It is probably too early to say what legacy the postmodern situation will leave to those who pray. At least three preliminary questions come to mind:

- To whom are we praying? This is the "New Age question" and one that arises naturally enough out of the integral worldview.
- What can we say is true about prayer? If knowledge is no longer universal but particular, can any claims be made for prayer that transcend the self?

- What is the power of speech to construe reality? If reality is not as linear and rigid as we have thought, if there is a spiritual element to all things, what is the power of speech to summon and shape an alternative to what is?

Let's look at each of these in turn.

To Whom Are We Praying?

Many Christians are both attracted to and repelled by the "New Age" agenda. The attraction stems from a sympathy to the integral worldview with its more organic understanding of reality. The repulsion stems from the recognition that there is little basis within this worldview for making an ultimate claim for the Judeo-Christian God. If Spirit is in all things, the reasoning seems to go, then I'll pick the thing that resonates most with me and make that the center of my worship. Thus, crystals, ecology, astrology, and even witchcraft (in both its hard and its soft forms) have an equally valid claim on supreme meaning. Both Brueggemann and Wink have a hint of what the default god of postmodernism will be. Brueggemann believes that, if we are not careful, consumerism will continue its dominance and become, even for the church, the dominant reality (1993:27). Wink's evaluation is more sweeping. He sees a "Domination System" and suggests that this system is nothing new, but goes back to the very beginning of civilization. This system of domination is "characterized by unjust economic relations, oppressive political relations, biased race relations, patriarchal gender relations, hierarchical power relations, and the use of violence to maintain them all" (39).

One thing is certain: Christianity can no longer rely on its Constantinian privilege of being the dominant cultural reality. Up against such heavy hitters as consumerism and the domination system, the only hope is in reclaiming the real spiritual power of our faith and offering it to a world that is beaten and abused by the alternatives. That *real power* lies in recovering *real prayer*.

What Can We Say Is True About Prayer?

One hallmark of postmodern reality is its plurality. In a previous time, some argue, truth was objective because it was the agreement of those who were "in the room," and very few people were admitted into the room. The demise of this objectivity came about as more people were slowly admitted to the room. Hence, objectivity is harder to maintain and eventually comes to be questioned. The new intellectual situation is to understand that knowledge is contextual—that is, what we know or see depends on where we are sitting in the room (Brueggemann 1993:8).

The inability to make universal claims may prove very troubling to Christianity. After almost two millennia of sitting at the head of the table, it is hard to suddenly be fighting for a place to stand in the room. In addition, since many Christians have bought into the "might makes right" mentality of the domination system, it is disorienting to suddenly be a beatitudinal church—meek, persecuted, and poor in spirit.

A quick study of the history of Christianity suggests, however, that the greatest progress has not been made by institutional statements of truth. Christian truth—in this case, the truth about prayer—is proved by the faithful lives of individuals. Jesus was clearly (and one might even suspect intentionally) outside of the existing power structures. Paul was not in much better shape. Nor have the great saints operated from a place of mass public influence. Rather, their lives were characterized by "prayer in action." They quietly went about living the gospel with enough integrity and commitment that it showed its own power and universal truth. If postmodern reality is such that only local and particular claims can now be made, then it is incumbent on each individual to be a disciple where he or she is, faithful in prayer toward the end of living out God's will in a particular place and time, and leaving the rest to God.

What Is the Power of Speech to Construe Reality?

One of the most intriguing and hopeful prospects for prayer growing out of the emerging postmodern understanding has to do with the power of speech to summon and shape an alternative reality. As Wink puts it, "history belongs to the intercessors" (185).

Such optimism grows out of the similarity between the ancient and the integral worldviews. Explicit in the former, and implicit in the latter, is the understanding that there is an inseparable connection between heaven and earth, between spirit and matter. It makes almost no sense, according to these worldviews, to speak of "spirit" and "matter." The whole universe, as noted earlier, is a spirit-matter event.

In such a worldview, speech takes on a significant role. "Speech is not merely descriptive," suggests Brueggemann, "but it is in some sense evocative of reality and constitutive of reality" (1993:12). In such a situation speech does more than describe; it gives voice to the work of imagination, which has the power to envision an alternative reality. Since the world is nothing more than an act of imagination that people have accepted as "real," it is open to a counterconstrual, one that imagines things could be different (13).

It is difficult, in this kind of conversation, to escape the spiritualist worldview, with its matter-denying proclivities. What is being argued is not that reality is merely an illusion (as in, for example, Mary Baker Eddy's "Christian Science"). Rather, what we call "reality" is a creation *ex nihilo* from a corporate imagination. We can prove this is so simply by looking at all the various realities there are in the world. Each group of people—European, African, Asian, male, female, poor, rich—has imagined its "world" differently. The dominance of one of these imagined worlds over another—by virtue of military, economic, or technological might—should not be misunderstood to mean that the dominant reality is therefore the most real.

This being the case, history does belong to the intercessors. Intercessors speak reality into being as cocreators with God, visualizing an alternative future. Wink notes that the "profound truth" of the ancient worldview is that "everything visible has an invisible or heavenly dimension"; for example, Revelation 8:1-5 suggests that when the saints on earth pray, the angels gather these prayers, mingle them with incense, and present them to God. The mixture is then thrown back to earth, which is shaken and convulsed as changes begin to take place (182). Says Wink, "The future belongs to whoever can envision a new and desirable possibility, which faith then fixes upon as inevitable" (185). There is great hope here, then, for reclaiming the power of prayer and meeting the challenges otherwise posed by the emerging postmodern "reality."

"How Can We Pray?" A Word on Mechanics

There are several things to be accomplished in this first class session. People may need to get to know one another, there will be a time to list concerns and questions, some initial definitions of prayer will be offered, and the territory ahead will be briefly charted. But we are gathered to learn to pray, and pray we must. This being the case, the class will be asked to covenant together to pray, which may raise some preliminary questions about the mechanics of prayer: *when, where,* and *how?*

When?

Asking busy people to carve out time to pray can threaten the fabric of polite society. While we sense the inherent truth that prayer is better for us than it is for God, restoring our energy and easing our tensions, few people will be able initially to connect this advice with their own action.

In asking for a prayer covenant we walk the line between discipline and guilt. Most Christians have enough guilt already, and it is generally a poor motivator. A call to healthy discipline is more promising. You might want to ask the class to brainstorm about times that might work. Some ideas might include rising fifteen minutes earlier, during lunch, or just before bed. The likelihood of holding firm is in direct proportion to the strength of anchor. Since most of us have few anchors in our daily schedules except getting up, eating, and going back to sleep, these may prove the strongest hopes.

Where?

The question of *when* will in most cases provide the answer to the question of *where*. Again, asking participants in the class for their ideas will spark and galvanize their thinking of a solution. Some ideas might include a quiet corner of the house early in the morning, the quiet solitude of one's car during lunch break, or the kitchen table after everyone else in the house has gone to bed. Some desperate soul may have to sit in the car in his or her own driveway in order to have a quiet place to go.

How?

This, of course, is the reason for the course! In each lesson we will introduce a new prayer skill, and the class should be encouraged to practice that skill and ones learned in preceding lessons during their prayer times. For this first week you might suggest that participants simply pray through the "Closing Prayer" handout, thus beginning to lay down the pattern of PRAYER in their hearts and minds.

Teaching the Class

The goal of this class is to begin forming relationships, to uncover any questions or concerns participants may have, to present some initial definitions of prayer, and to overview what is coming in the remaining weeks of this study.

❖ **Greet participants and share names** *(5 minutes).*

❖ **Open in prayer.**

❖ **Introduction** *(5 minutes)*

One way to give this introduction might be to say something like this:

> "Over the past several years there has been a great surge in the market for various books for novices. Many of these are tied to the computer industry, but it seems that for just about every topic imaginable there is now a basic book telling people how to do whatever it is.
>
> "Part of the reassurance of these books lies in the very title. 'This book,' we say to ourselves, 'isn't going to have a bunch of words in it that I won't understand. It's going to take me through the learning process one step at a time.'
>
> "That's what this class is about. While we didn't choose to call it *Prayer for Dummies* for pastoral reasons (!), it amounts to essentially that. You aren't expected to know anything, except perhaps that you have a deep longing for God, and that is the best beginning of all for any talk about prayer.
>
> "With that as reassurance, let's share the questions, concerns, and barriers we bring to the group. We all promise that there are no stupid questions, that we will not laugh, that we are all here to learn, and that we are all beginners."

❖ **List questions, concerns, and barriers** *(5-10 minutes).*

You may need to prompt participants with some of your own, such as:

32

Does God hear all my prayers?
Why do some prayers go unanswered?
Do I have to pray with my eyes closed?

Be sure to save these questions for reference in chapter 7.

❖ **Distribute prayer definitions** *(10-15 minutes).*

Distribute the handout entitled "Some Definitions of Prayer."
Read it or invite someone else to read it aloud, briefly discussing
the material as the group's interest leads. Although there is no single "right" definition, it may emerge that prayer is less about
speech than about relationship.

❖ **Overview PRAYER** *(5-10 minutes).*

Distribute the handout entitled "PRAYER." *Briefly* say a word
or two about each movement. Don't try to do too much, and reassure people not to panic about what they don't understand. The
purpose here is to quickly survey the road ahead. You might want
to say something like this:

"In this class we will learn a way of praying based on the
acronym PRAYER. This acronym is based on the model
given to us by Jesus in the Lord's Prayer, which we will look
at next week. We'll then spend a week on each of these six
movements in prayer.

"The first movement is called **Psalming** and simply suggests that we start our prayer time using a prayer from
Psalms, the prayer book of the Bible. We'll spend some time
learning about the different kinds of psalms and how they
can help us pray. The second movement in prayer is
Reconciling, a time for us to confess and seek forgiveness
from God and anyone else with whom we are unreconciled.
Adoring is a time in prayer for us to give praise and thanks
for all God has done for us. In this same lesson we'll learn
about different styles of prayer that correlate to different personality types.

"It doesn't make sense that in our relationship with God
we do all the talking, so the next move of prayer may be the

most important. **Yielding** is a time for us to be still and know God, to listen for God's voice. In this lesson we'll talk about ways to discern if what we hear in prayer is of God. **Entreating** is the next movement of prayer. It is here that we finally get to ask God about those things that concern us, whether on behalf of ourselves or on behalf of others. The last move of prayer might be called "prayer-shaped action." It is **Realizing** the ongoing relationship we have with God as we go about living our lives. Some have called this practicing the presence; Paul called it praying without ceasing.

❖ Distribute Covenants *(5-10 minutes)*.

Explain to the class that these covenants are between themselves and God: no one else will look at them. Explain further that after they have completed their covenants, they should fold the sheet twice. During the closing prayer there will be an opportunity to offer the covenants as a "Realized" form of prayer. It would be good to have a supply of pens and pencils for class members to use, and you may want to use an offering plate to collect the covenants during the prayer.

While people are filling out the covenants, lead a brief conversation on the *when, where, how* questions.

❖ Closing Prayer *(5 minutes)*

Tell the class that each week will include an opportunity to experience what we are learning—it doesn't make a lot of sense to talk about prayer without actually doing some of it! Distribute "Closing Prayer" sheets and lead the closing prayer.

❖ At Home This Week

Ask participants to work toward fulfilling their covenants and suggest that they can use the "Closing Prayer" as the basis for their prayer time for the coming week.

Some Definitions of Prayer

"Prayer is an offering up of our desires unto God, for things agreeable to his will, in the name of Christ, with confession of our sins, and thankful acknowledgment of his mercies." (*The Shorter Catechism*, Question 98)[3]

"Prayer is the nearest approach to God and the highest enjoyment of him that we are capable of in this life." (William Law, *A Serious Call to a Devout and Holy Life*, p. 91)

"Prayer in its essence is neither fear, nor social control, nor auto-suggestion, nor rationalization. The certitude abides that it is comradeship with God." (George A. Buttrick, *Prayer*, p. 53)

"The chief purpose of prayer is to meet with God and to have fellowship with Him. Many adult Christians have not advanced beyond the point of childhood petitions, when prayer, taught at Mother's knee, consisted of a short list of wants and intercessions for loved ones. While 'God bless Mummy and Daddy' is a lovely prayer for a child of five, it has little in it to feed the soul of a man of forty-five. Prayer that contains little more than a list of requests reflects small credit either on God or us. It is a paltry and crudely acquisitive spirit that clamours for gifts and never pauses to think of the Giver." (W. E. Sangster, *The Pattern of Prayer*, p. 16)

"Prayer is an experience of pure trust and loving obedience which elevates even a modest life when truly related to the Living God." (Elton Trueblood, *The Lord's Prayers*, pp. 13-14)

"Christianity is not a religion; it is a relationship. And a relationship requires communication. . . . There are countless decisions to be made, wisdom to be sought, resources that are needed, transgressions to be mended, love and appreciation to be communicated. Thus, we are told to pray without ceasing . . . to talk with and listen to our heavenly Father. This is prayer." (Kay Arthur, *Lord, Teach Me to Pray in 28 Days*, p. 6)

Prayer

Psalming

Reconciling

Adoring

Yielding

Entreating

Realizing

Covenant

Trusting in the grace and forgiveness and power of God, I covenant to do my best to do the following:

_____ Attend each of the eight class sessions

_____ Have a time of prayer

_____daily

_____every other day

_____weekly

Signed_____

Closing Prayer

*P*SALMING

Leader: *I love you, O* LORD, *my strength.*

Group: The LORD is my rock, my fortress, and my deliverer, my God, my rock in whom I take refuge, my shield, and the horn of my salvation, my stronghold.

Leader: *I call upon the* LORD, *who is worthy to be praised,*

Group: so I shall be saved from my enemies. (Ps. 18:1-3)

*R*ECONCILING

Leader: *Hear us, O God, as we silently remember and tell you the things we have done that we should not have done . . .* (pause) *and those things we have not done that we should have done.* (pause)

*A*DORING *(in unison)*

O the depth of the riches and wisdom and knowledge of God! How unsearchable are his judgments and how inscrutable his ways! "For who has known the mind of the Lord? Or who has been his counselor?" "Or who has given a gift to him, to receive a gift in return?" For from him and through him and to him are all things. To him be the glory forever. (Rom. 11:33-36)

*Y*IELDING *(silent listening)*

ENTREATING

Leader:	*Let us pray for peace, which is Heaven's gift.*
Group:	May the Lord in his mercy give us peace.
Leader:	*Let us pray for faith.*
Group:	May the Lord give us grace to keep our faith in him untainted to the end.
Leader:	*Let us pray for unity of hearts and minds.*
Group:	May the Lord keep our minds and hearts as one.
Leader:	*Let us pray for patience.*
Group:	In all our afflictions may the Lord grant us patience to the end.
Leader:	*Let us pray for the whole world.*
Group:	May the Lord provide for all creatures and give to each what is best for it. (Liturgical Fragment, third century)

REALIZING *(place covenants in the offering plate)*

Chapter Two

The Lord's Prayer as Pattern

There are few things about worship in the mainline tradition more disheartening than a congregation racing blindly through the Lord's Prayer as it ticks off the next item on the worship agenda. The irony is extraordinary. In his most concise teaching on prayer Jesus warns his disciples against praying empty, repetitive prayers. He then offers a pattern prayer, as was commonly done by teachers in his day. His followers, ourselves included, apparently ignored the first part of the instruction and seized upon the latter, which gave rise to the obligatory use of the Lord's Prayer, no matter how empty or repetitive.

But what then are we to do—abandon the Lord's Prayer completely? This action hardly seems likely or desirable. This prayer has been so important to so many people for so long. In fact, in the early church, the Lord's Prayer was not an "open prayer" but was instead reserved for the baptized community, those who had completed the three-year training required to become a Christian. Only those who had been adopted through Christ as God's children could rightfully pray to God as "Father" (Lochman, 14).

We value the words of Jesus as delivered by scripture, and we sense in the Lord's Prayer a depth and precision that our praying will likely never achieve. And so, if we are preachers, we do the Lord's Prayer sermon series once every few years, and if we are laity, we suffer through the same in the hope that somehow the prayer we know should mean a lot to us finally will. And then, the week or the month after the series ends, we once more race (or plod) through the prayer, the legacy of the recent series leaving only a heightened sense of guilt because the prayer still doesn't mean much to us.

The mistake, it seems, is that we typically examine the Lord's Prayer for content only. But the Lord's Prayer is both content *and* pattern, which explains how Jesus could make his comments

41

about repetition and then go on and offer a model prayer. When Jesus said, "Pray then *in this way* . . . ," the *in this way* meant "in this manner" as much as it meant "with these words." Once we understand not only the meaning of Jesus' words but also the reality that these words point us to various topics, we are free to use Jesus' model as a jumping-off spot to prayer of our own. "Prayer modeled after the Lord's Prayer is the ever-new beginning of our participation in the work of God in the world. It is the beginning of active partnership with God who wills to be God with us, not apart from us" (Migliore 1993:2).

What is the content of the Lord's Prayer, and how can we use recent insights to better understand that content? What is the pattern of the Lord's Prayer, and what does this pattern have to say concerning the idea that "the medium is the message"? Finally, how can we engage our own creativity to use the shape and content of the Lord's Prayer to give shape and content to our own prayers?

The Content of the Lord's Prayer

"Our Father which art in heaven"

Some wonderful insights have emerged in recent scholarship pertaining to the content of the Lord's Prayer. Leading among these is Roberta Bondi's reflective book *A Place to Pray*. She takes the lead on the messy business of saying "Our Father" in a culture sensitized by the insights of feminism. No matter what Jesus may have meant or understood, we may question saying "Our Father" when patriarchal images have been used to strengthen the authority and power of men in the church, often at the expense of women.

One response is to give those who have been hurt or abused by fathers or men the freedom and the space to pray using a different image. Bondi is personally familiar with the special needs of this population. At the same time, however, she challenges the notion that Jesus ever shared in the authoritative agenda of a male hegemony. "Jesus never told women, or men either, much less poor or oppressed people, to knuckle under and accept the status quo as God's powerful 'will' for them," suggests Bondi. "As I read it, Jesus' teaching about God's fatherhood is just as subversive. I challenge anybody to find a place where Jesus uses God's fatherhood to shore up human male authority, including the authority of our own fathers" (14). Jesus' agenda, far from supporting an abusive status quo, was to turn things on their heads, and this is what saying "Our Father" can communicate.

Beyond this, of course, is the fairly familiar notion that saying "Our Father" is to say all that needs to be said. The early Christian father Chrysostom indicated that to say these words was "to confess one's faith in the forgiveness of sins, remission of punishment, justification, sanctification, redemption, adoption as a child of God, an heir, a sibling of the Only-Begotten, enjoying the communion of the Holy Spirit" (quoted in Froehlich, 76).

Finally, the use of the first person plural "*Our* Father," not only here but also throughout the prayer, is a good reminder that the Christian faith is radically social. As noted in the introduction, there is a distinct difference between faith that is nourishingly personal and faith that is anemically private. This communal nature of faith will also become important when we deal with Reconciling, understanding that God is both my Father and the Father of my enemy.

"Hallowed be thy name"

The phrase is troubling on two counts. First is the archaic language of "hallowed." Hardly better is "holied be your name,"[1] but it gets us closer to the second, more significant idea: that somehow God is made more holy by our prayer. One asks immediately if this prayer is for God or for us, but we dare not be too quick to answer. For if we say that it is for us, we lay the foundation for a critique of prayer as merely psychological suggestion. Prayer, in this view, doesn't accomplish much in any material sense, but it at least reminds us who we are compared to this holy God. If, on the other hand, we take seriously an integral worldview in which prayer does affect and change things, then we are faced with a truth almost too much to bear. Either God's name and nature are, to use the language of the psalmist, "magnified" in our prayers or, because we haven't prayed, God is somehow diminished, not just in our psyches, but materially. This may be going down theological roads we'd rather not take, but we must wrestle with what this petition means and why Jesus would include it.

A less controversial understanding of the phrase is offered by Bondi when she says that "real prayer is a conversation with God which, as much as we might like to, we can't really script to suit ourselves." When we pray for God's name to be hallowed, then we are praying for God to be Who God Is and not simply the God Whom We Would Prefer. When God is hallowed in our prayer, really and materially, "we can't assign God's lines in advance, get God to recite them in our minds, and then say we've had an actual conversation, or gotten any genuinely new insight" (32). To hallow, make holy, and magnify God's name is to constantly take God outside our control.

"Thy kingdom come"

Although this phrase and the one following, "thy will be done," are traditionally treated as two petitions, a case can be made that they are, in fact, speaking to the same end. That Jesus would use this kind of parallelism isn't surprising. Still, like all good parallelism, the two phrases give us slightly different castings of the core idea, namely, that all our wishes and desires are first subject to God's will.

Once again addressing the negative overtones of dominance our culture tends to read into such words as "kingdom," Bondi suggests that:

> God's kingdom, which comes according to God's will, is a gift, not a nightmare of coercion. God desires our life and not our death. "Do you not realize," Jesus asks us, "that God's kingdom is where God's will is done, and that God's will for you is for your well-being, and for the well-being of all God has created? This is the Kingdom you pray for. If you live in this awareness, then as far as it is possible in this world, you can live now in the Kingdom." (61)

"Thy will be done in earth, as it is in heaven"

This petition, even more than the one preceding, seems to get at the heart of what we would want to pray. Picking up on the notion articulated above by Bondi, a healthy theology of prayer recognizes that God wants what is best for us even more than we want it ourselves. Although our prayers may not always give voice to what is best for us, we are encouraged to pray them anyway—such is the love of the Father. But having expressed our deepest longings, we finally fall exhausted into the loving arms of God's embrace, saying, "Your will be done."[2]

A more intriguing question raised by this petition is why it is here in the first place. The view of Enlightenment superheated Calvinism is that God's will is always going to be done. While we may be comforted by this thought, and while it may hold up in the end (which is to say, eschatologically), we must take seriously the fact that God's will isn't always done. How many times has a pastor stood beside a hospital bed and heard the patient say, "I know God must have a reason for this"? The implicit theological assumption is that everything that happens, happens for a reason—namely, that God wills it. We may avoid the idea that some things happen outside of God's control, but this avoidance comes at the cost of a more frightening assertion: that God wills sickness, tragedy, and disease "for a reason."

To pray "thy will be done" is to enter into alliance with God against a common enemy. If God is our friend and wills the best for us, then we must admit the possibility of a third player, what the Bible calls "principalities and powers" and what Walter Wink calls "the powers that be." However these others are to be understood, we must move to a worldview that makes room for them if praying "thy will be done" is to make any sense at all.

"Give us this day our daily bread"

Most scholars recognize a break in the prayer at this point. The previous petitions have dealt with "what God may properly expect from us"; the following petitions deal with "what we may properly expect God to do for us" (Purdy, 2-3).

It is possible to spiritualize the petition for daily bread, but such interpretation seems overdone. Besides the wonderfully comforting permission of being able to pray for such "unspiritual" things as bread (and by extension, other basic human needs such as shelter and clothing), the petition for bread fires the imagination by using the word "daily." It is hard to consider this word without thinking about the nature of manna, which lasted only the day and then rotted. To be daily dependent on God's provision for the basics of life is a reality most of us don't know. Still, it is a reminder to us not to worry and fret over our bread—pension plans, CDs, and IRAs.

"And forgive us our debts, as we forgive our debtors"

Without getting bogged down in the relative merits of "debts," "trespasses," or "sins," let us agree that the focus of the petition is on forgiveness. We will be devoting an entire chapter to this subject ("Reconciling"), but it is interesting to note that in Jesus' "hierarchy of needs" forgiveness follows daily bread!

Just as interesting is the fact that, of all the petitions in the Lord's Prayer, this is the only one on which Jesus made further comment (Matt. 6:14-15). The apparent significance of forgiveness for us is magnified by our Enlightenment heritage. "What does the world need more than the power that overcomes this curse of debt? . . . For the reality of debt and the reality of forgiveness are too vast and at the same time too mysterious to be mastered by man with his calculating mind and his achievements of power in manufacturing and technology" (Ebeling, 73). In other words, while we may not have much concern about daily bread, daily forgiveness is a place where we all live.

"And lead us not into temptation, but deliver us from evil"

Once more, the phrasing of this petition gives us all kinds of difficult theological questions. Is God the one who tempts us? And if it is not God, then does God nevertheless allow us to be tempted?

One solution is offered by biblical scholar James Charlesworth, who is convinced that Jesus taught the Lord's

Prayer in Aramaic. If this was the case, the Aramaic translation of this petition works out to "do not allow us to enter into temptation," a translation that is in sympathy with the way in which most commentators take the meaning anyway (see James 1:13) (Charlesworth, 48).

A second solution moves past artificial discussion of who is responsible for temptation and recognizes that we are ultimately responsible for our own actions. The point of this petition is then seen clearly in terms of preparedness, and so Elton Trueblood suggests that if we wait to pray to avoid temptation at the time we are facing temptation, it is already too late! "Unless we arm ourselves in advance of the moral battle," says Trueblood, "we have very little chance when finally the actual test occurs. . . . Our best chance of escape from moral danger . . . lies in the act of prayerful preparedness." Trueblood then quotes Professor John Baillie, who said that sin is conquered "not in the moment of temptation but in the long prayerful discipline that precedes it" (60-61).

A slightly different solution is offered by Richard Foster, who sees in this petition a plea for cleansing. God uses trial and temptation to reveal to us what is in our hearts that still needs to be purified. Thus, he suggests that Jesus may have intended something like, "Lord, may there be nothing in me that will force you to put me to the test in order to reveal what is in my heart" (189).

*"For thine is the kingdom, and the power,
and the glory, for ever"*

Scholars have long recognized that these words were not originally part of the prayer that Jesus gave to his disciples. Yet they also recognize that they are a fitting note of praise and adoration.

The importance of adoration would be hard to overstate. The psalmist suggests that it is the way by which we come into the presence of God: "Enter his gates with thanksgiving, and his courts with praise" (Ps. 100:4). The suggestion here, and indeed throughout scripture, is that we come closer to God as we give praise and thanksgiving.

In his devotional classic *A Serious Call to a Devout and Holy Life*, William Law indicates that if anyone would tell us "the shortest, surest way to all happiness and all perfection, he must tell you to make a rule to yourself to thank and praise God for everything that happens to you. If you could work miracles," says Law, "you could not do more for yourself than by this thankful spirit. It heals and turns all that it touches into happiness" (101).

The words seem overly simple, and so they may be in some extreme cases. On the other hand, most of us would do well to have the attitude of a certain young husband who took his wife's car to get her a bagel while she was in labor. When he stopped, the axle broke. Rather than fuss about the inconvenient timing or the bother of getting the car repaired with everything else going on, his sincere praise was, "Thank God she wasn't driving it at top speed this past week!"

The Lord's Prayer as Pattern

The content of the Lord's Prayer is, of course, only part of its lesson for us. It is generally well recognized that rabbis in Jesus' day encouraged spontaneous prayers. Given the context of the prayer, offered as it is after Jesus' words against ostentatious Gentile prayer, it seems clear that the Lord's Prayer was meant to be a model for personal spontaneous prayer (Charlesworth, 47-48).

At the very least we should consider the Lord's Prayer to be a kind of bidding prayer (this will be its use in the closing prayer for this lesson) in which each petition suggests a subject for prayer. In this way the prayer can be used much more reflectively in personal devotions than it is in public worship. If as individuals we were to say one petition at a time, pause to remember the type of prayer it represented, and then pray our own prayer of this type, it would go far toward enriching our corporate use of the Lord's Prayer.

Numerous suggestions have been made for understanding and categorizing the various petitions in the prayer. Three contemporary authors who have done work with the *pattern* of the Lord's Prayer are Larry Lea *(Could You Not Tarry One Hour?)*, John C. Purdy *(Lord, Teach Us to Pray)*, and Kay Arthur *(Lord, Teach Me to Pray in 28 Days)*. The chart below summarizes their insights.[3]

Petition	Larry Lea	John C. Purdy	Kay Arthur
Our Father which art in heaven, hallowed be thy name.	God's promises	respect for God's holiness	worship
Thy kingdom come	God's priorities	commitment to the coming kingdom	allegiance
Thy will be done in earth, as it is in heaven	(included above)	obedience to God's law in our lives	submission
Give us this day our daily bread	God's provision	satisfaction of our physical needs	petition/ intercession
And forgive us our debts, as we forgive our debtors	God's people	liberation from our bondage to sin	confession
And lead us not into temptation, but deliver us from evil	God's power	deliverance from the powers of evil	deliverance
For thine is the kingdom, and the power, and the glory, for ever.	(not referenced)	(not referenced)	worship

Among other things, the chart shows that no one scheme neatly includes every part or gets to the heart of each petition in a clear and memorable way. The most satisfying of these is the one presented by Larry Lea. But even this fails somewhat in the category of memorability.

The model being offered in this study scores high marks for memorability—what could be easier to remember when one is trying to pray than the word PRAYER? If it has a drawback, it is in the reorganization of the pattern. Thus:

*P*salming   Our Father which art in heaven, hallowed be thy name.

*R*econciling   And forgive us our debts, as we forgive our debtors.

*A*doring   For thine is the kingdom, and the power, and the glory, for ever.

*Y*ielding   Thy kingdom come. Thy will be done in earth, as it is in heaven.

*E*ntreating   Give us this day our daily bread.

*R*ealizing   And lead us not into temptation, but deliver us from evil.

Can We Do This?

The first issue that needs to be addressed is whether a defense can be made for such reordering. There can certainly be teased out of the ordering of the Lord's Prayer an implicit theological statement concerning the right order of prayer. According to this understanding, the first three petitions of the prayer look directly to God. Only after God has been "rendered God's due" are we then free to move to the second three petitions, which look to human needs.

While this sounds good in theory, the actual practice of prayer suggests something else. The short, emotional, ejaculatory phrases that Heiler and others consider to be the truest kind of prayer usually grow out of our point of need at the moment. Thus, prayers such as "Help," "I'm sorry," and even "Wow!" (a postmodern prayer of praise) find their way from our lips without any consideration of theological propriety. Moreover, to think that God would reject our prayer simply because we didn't pray it in the right order, or didn't appease God's ego at the outset, is to postulate a God too small to hear most prayers.

As we will see in the next chapter ("Psalming"), there is both an order and a disorder to the prayers in Psalms. Although the psalms have identifiable elements according to their type, these elements rarely proceed in an orderly fashion. The more intense the emotion of the psalm, the more likely we are to find it darting back and forth from complaint to trust, from petition to praise, and then back to complaint once more.

A goal of this study is to move people past the fear and insecurity of thinking that there is a "right way" to pray, some kind of magic formula that, if we can only master it, will require God to act in the ways we desire. It is much more in keeping with an understanding of God's relationship with us as Father that we should feel the freedom to pour out our hearts in a random manner. And if these are imperfect offerings (which is doubtful), we can as a last refuge know that the Holy Spirit gathers these prayers and "tidies them up," interceding for us.

The primary consideration, then, is not the order but the completeness of our praying. The PRAYER acronym provides an easy-to-remember checklist of where we've been and what we need yet to do in prayer. Moreover, class members will be reminded again in the final lesson that they needn't be slave to the order; instead, they are guided by it to include all of the appropriate parts of prayer.

Do These Parts Fit?

The second issue to be addressed is whether or not the letters of the suggested acronym actually fit the various parts of the Lord's Prayer. The answer is that some are clearer than others. It is not difficult to connect Reconciling with the phrase "And forgive us our debts, as we forgive our debtors"; to connect Entreating with the phrase "Give us this day our daily bread"; or to connect Adoring with the closing doxological ascription "For thine is the kingdom, and the power, and the glory, for ever." Let's look for a moment at the others.

The suggestion that something called "Psalming" can be found in the phrase "Our Father which art in heaven, hallowed be thy name" asks first for a definition of Psalming. Simply stated, Psalming is a term that refers to the long tradition of drawing on the prayers we find in the psalter as a starting place for our own praying. The discipline of various monastic traditions includes reading through the entire psalter at least monthly, if not more often. Our approach is not nearly so rigorous: it simply suggests that we start our prayer time by reading a psalm, either in sequence or perhaps by type (lament, well-being, or thanksgiving), according to our needs at the moment.

Whether or not the practice of Psalming can be found in the first petition of the Lord's Prayer is a fair question, and one that perhaps can't be answered persuasively. What can be said with certainty is that the psalter was the prayer book of Jesus, and virtually every petition in the Lord's Prayer can be found in some form in one of the psalms (see the "Opening Litany" exercise for chapter 3).

A similar set of questions arises for Yielding: What is meant by the word, and can that meaning be found in "Thy kingdom come. Thy will be done in earth, as it is in heaven"? "Yielding" is a word that suggests we take seriously the *dialogical* character of prayer. Thus, prayer must include a time for being still, for listening, for waiting on God. If in prayer we are the only ones doing the talking, we have missed out on the meaning of prayer as conversation, and more tragically, we have missed the chance to hear from our God.

It is only as we listen, then, that we can begin to know what God's kingdom and will might look like here on earth. Stillness is our only hope for recognizing the pearl of great price that is the kingdom—quietude our only hope to hear the birds in the tree that grew from the tiniest seed. To ask for God's kingdom to come and will to be done is, therefore, to presuppose that we have heard enough about these things from God's own lips, as we wait patiently for the ever-spoken Word.

"Realizing" is the enactment of our prayer, a living out of what our conversation with God has brought to the fore. Practicing the presence, praying without ceasing, and the very nature of the spiritual life are not determined solely by the time we spend on our knees, but by the corresponding time we spend being Christ's hands and feet.

To suggest that the phrase "And lead us not into temptation, but deliver us from evil" gets us to this move in prayer is again open to question. A rationale could perhaps be found in the idea that it is most likely in our engagement of the world that we meet temptations and evils. To "realize" the spiritual life is much harder as we face these trials and temptations than it is in the relative safety of the prayer closet.

Creative Engagement with the Lord's Prayer

Knowing both the content and the shape of the Lord's Prayer will go a long way toward helping us use the prayer as it was intended: as a catalyst for our own prayers. Thus, instead of saying the entire prayer in one sitting, we might find ourselves praying "hallowed be thy name" again and again, drawing out the wonder of God's holiness, looking through the psalms for the great scenes of the heavenly court arrayed in its full splendor, and focusing the whole morning while at work on living as God's holy child. At noon we might move to "Give us this day our daily bread" as we say the blessing over our lunch, and then proceed, with each bite, to entreat God for the various concerns of our hearts. A midafternoon sight of clouds drenched in sunlight or of a single flower braving the urban environment might give us pause to say with adoration, "For thine is the kingdom, and the power, and the glory, for ever," and from that point continue in an attitude of thanksgiving and praise for the rest of the day. With any grace at all, as the hours unfold, we'll be able to find quiet moments to Yield, listening to that still small voice guide us throughout the day. In a reflective moment after dinner or before bedtime we might become aware of our angers and frustrations from the day, leading to a time of fruitful forgiveness and repentance. All of these inputs—the positive ones as well as the temptations and trials of the day—will have helped our prayer to be Realized, God's presence practiced, and conversation with God offered without ceasing.

That's the theory, anyway. The reality is that we may faithfully meet God for a morning devotion and then go the entire day without another prayerful thought—and this even if we are God's people ostensibly doing holy things all day long!

Teaching the Class

The goals of this session are to overview the Lord's Prayer in both content and pattern, and to show the relationship of the Lord's Prayer to the PRAYER outline we'll be using for the remainder of the classes.

❖ **Opening Prayer** *(5 minutes)*

Distribute the handout entitled "The Lord's Prayer" and pray it together twice as a group, using at least two different versions (for example, Matthew and Ecumenical).

❖ **Discuss the *content* of the Lord's Prayer** *(15-20 minutes)*.

Use one of the following methods to overview the content of the Lord's Prayer:
♦ Ask participants to talk about what each petition means.
♦ Work through a catechistic presentation on the Lord's Prayer (one is included, or use a denominational resource).
♦ Present your own overview of highlights as more of a lecture.

❖ **Discuss the *pattern* of the Lord's Prayer** *(15-20 minutes)*.

Move the discussion from content to pattern by asking participants to read and reflect on Matthew 6:5-8. Ask participants how we can reconcile Jesus' words here regarding repetitive prayers and the way we typically use the Lord's Prayer.

Suggest that part of the solution might be to understand the Lord's Prayer as a *pattern* for prayer as much as it is a prayer. If your tradition uses bidding prayers in worship, you should be able to make this point with ease.

Distribute the worksheet entitled "A Pattern for Prayer." Ask participants to fill in the second column using the various phrasings from "The Lord's Prayer" worksheet, one petition of the Lord's Prayer per block on the chart. Provide guidance using the material found below ("Closing Prayer" exercise).

❖ **Overview PRAYER** *(5-10 minutes).*

As you have time and need, make a case for this reordering using the material in the section of chapter 2 entitled "Can We Do This?"

❖ **Closing Prayer**

Lead a bidding prayer in which the lines of the Lord's Prayer are offered by the leader one by one, each followed by a period of silence. Participants are invited to silently pray for those areas or topics named by the petition of the Lord's Prayer being offered. For an added degree of thoughtfulness, leaders may want to offer the petitions of the Lord's Prayer in the order suggested by the PRAYER outline, thus:

P Our Father which art in heaven, hallowed be thy name.

R And forgive us our debts, as we forgive our debtors.

A For thine is the kingdom, and the power, and the glory, for ever.

Y Thy kingdom come. Thy will be done in earth, as it is in heaven.

E Give us this day our daily bread.

R And lead us not into temptation, but deliver us from evil.

❖ **At Home This Week**

Encourage participants to work with the Lord's Prayer as a pattern for their prayers, letting each petition suggest an area or category for their extended praying.

The Lord's Prayer

"Our Father in heaven, hallowed be your name. Your kingdom come. Your will be done, on earth as it is in heaven. Give us this day our daily bread. And forgive us our debts, as we also have forgiven our debtors. And do not bring us to the time of trial, but rescue us from the evil one." (Matt. 6:9-13)

"Father, hallowed be your name. Your kingdom come. Give us each day our daily bread. And forgive us our sins, for we ourselves forgive everyone indebted to us. And do not bring us to the time of trial." (Luke 11:2-4)

"Our Father which art in heaven, Hallowed be thy name. Thy kingdom come. Thy will be done in earth, as it is in heaven. Give us this day our daily bread. And forgive us our debts, as we forgive our debtors. And lead us not into temptation, but deliver us from evil: For thine is the kingdom, and the power, and the glory, for ever." (Traditional, KJV)

"Our Father in heaven, hallowed be your name. Your kingdom come. Your will be done, on earth as in heaven. Give us today our daily bread. Forgive us our sins as we forgive those who sin against us. Save us from the time of trial and deliver us from evil. For the kingdom, the power, and the glory are yours now and for ever." (Ecumenical)[4]

Questions and Answers
on the Lord's Prayer from
The Study Catechism
of the Presbyterian Church (USA)

Question 126. *What is meant by addressing God as "Our Father in heaven"?*

By addressing God as "our Father," we draw near with childlike reverence, and place ourselves securely in God's hands. Although God is certainly everywhere, God is said to exist and dwell "in heaven." For while God is free to enter into the closest relationship with the creature, God does not belong to the order of created beings. "Heaven" is the seat of divine authority, the place from which God reigns in glory and brings salvation to earth. Our opening address expresses our confidence that we rest securely in God's intimate care, and that nothing on earth lies beyond the reach of God's grace.

Question 127. *What is meant by the first petition, "Hallowed be your name"?*

This petition is placed first, because it comprehends the goal and purpose of the whole prayer. The glory of God's name is the highest concern in all that we pray and do. God's "name" stands for God's being as well as for God's attributes and works. When we pray for this name to be "hallowed," we ask that we and all others will know and glorify God as God really is, and that all things will be so ordered that they serve God truly for God's sake.

Question 128. *What is meant by the second petition, "Your kingdom come"?*

We are asking God to come and rule among us through faith, love and justice—and not through any one of them without the others. We pray for both the church and the world, that God will rule in our hearts through faith, in our personal relationships through love, and in our institutional affairs through justice. We ask especially that the gospel will not be withheld from us, but rightly preached and received. We pray that the church will be upheld and increase, particularly when in distress; and that all the world will more and more submit to God's reign, until that day when crying and pain are no more, and we live forever with God in perfect peace.

Question 129. *What is meant by the third petition, "Your will be done, on earth as in heaven"?*

Of course, God's will is always done, and will surely come to pass, whether we desire it or not. But the phrase "on earth as in heaven" means that we ask for the grace to do God's will on earth in the *way* that it is done in heaven—gladly and from the heart. We thus ask that all opposition to God's will might be removed from the earth, and especially from our own hearts. We ask for the freedom to conform our desires and deeds more fully to God's, so that we might be completely delivered from our sin. We yield ourselves, in life and in death, to God's will.

Question 130. *What is meant by the fourth petition, "Give us today our daily bread"?*

We ask God to provide for all our needs, for we know that God, who cares for us in every area of our life, has promised us temporal as well as spiritual blessings. God commands us to pray each day for all that we need and no more, so that we will learn to rely completely on God. We pray that we will use what we are given wisely, remembering especially the poor and the needy. Along with every living creature we look to God, the source of all generosity, to bless us and nourish us, according to the divine good pleasure.

Question 131. *What is meant by the fifth petition, "Forgive us our sins as we forgive those who sin against us"?*

We pray that a new and right spirit will be put within us. We ask for the grace to treat others, especially those who harm us, with the same mercy that we have received from God. We remember that not one day goes by when we do not need to turn humbly to God for our own forgiveness. We know that our reception of this forgiveness can be blocked by our unwillingness to forgive others. We ask that we will not delight in doing evil, nor in avenging any wrong, but that we will survive all cruelty without bitterness, and overcome evil with good, so that our hearts will be knit together with the mercy and forgiveness of God.

Question 132. *What is meant by the final petition, "Save us from the time of trial and deliver us from evil"?*

We ask God to protect us from our own worst impulses and from all external powers of destruction in the world. We ask that we might not yield to despair in the face of seemingly hopeless circumstances. We pray for the grace to remember and believe, despite our unbelief, that no matter how bleak the world may sometimes seem, there is nonetheless a depth of love which is deeper than our despair, and that this love—which delivered Israel from slavery in Egypt and raised our Lord Jesus from the dead—will finally swallow up forever all that would now seem to defeat it.

Question 133. *What is meant by the closing doxology, "For the kingdom, the power, and the glory are yours now and for ever"?*

We give God thanks and praise for the kingdom more powerful than all enemies, for the power perfected in the weakness of love, and for the glory that includes our well-being and that of the whole creation, both now and to all eternity. We give thanks and praise to God as made known through Christ our Lord.

Question 134. *What is meant by the word, "Amen"?*

"Amen" means "so be it" or "let it be so." It expresses our complete confidence in the triune God, the God of the covenant with Israel as fulfilled through our Lord Jesus Christ, who makes no promise that will not be kept, and whose steadfast love and mercy endures forever.

A Pattern for Prayer

PRAYER	Which petition do you think fits?
Psalming	
Reconciling	
Adoring	
Yielding	
Entreating	
Realizing	

Chapter Three
Psalming

The psalms were the foundation of Jesus' prayer life. Like any good Jew of his day, Jesus would have memorized large sections of the psalter, which provided a default language for prayer. On the cross, in the midst of unspeakable physical suffering, this default language emerges as Jesus prays, "My God, my God, why have you forsaken me?" (Ps. 22:1*a*), and "Into your hand I commit my spirit" (Ps. 31:5*a*).

"Psalming" is also apparent throughout the pattern prayer that Jesus gave us (see the "Opening Litany" for this session). If Jesus' own prayer life was so rooted in the psalms, it is also fitting for ours to be rooted and grounded in the prayer book of the Bible.

In his devotional classic, *A Serious Call to a Devout and Holy Life*, William Law suggests that all prayer should begin with a psalm. "There is nothing that so clears a way for your prayers," says Law, "nothing that so disperses dullness of heart, nothing that so purifies the soul from poor and little passions, nothing that so opens heaven or carries your heart so near it as these songs of praise." For Law, as for Christians throughout the ages, the psalms "kindle a holy flame; they turn your heart into an altar; they turn your prayers into incense and carry them as sweet-smelling savor to the throne of grace" (98).

But those of us coming for the first time to take a serious look at the psalms may be somewhat frustrated. In part this is due to the wide variety of psalms, their apparently hodgepodge order, and their apparently nonlinear flow.[1] A handout for the class, which is included at the end of the chapter, offers a list of "user-friendly" psalms that should help class members easily find prayable psalms before branching off into more difficult areas.

A second reason for the frustration presented by the psalms has to do with a misconception. What we typically hear offered in public worship are carefully crafted linear prayers that intimidate us into believing that *this* is the way to pray. Fortunately, the psalms correct this misconception by offering a way of praying that is more true to the cry of the human soul, a way of praying that cycles around and around between praise, petition, lament, and vows of trust. Once we get past looking for crafted, linear prayers in the psalms, we are freed to borrow them as our own, to use them as a humble offering to God from "out of the depths"—in groanings and sighs too deep for words, in prayers that we trust the Spirit to put into whatever shape they need be for presentation at the throne of God.

Psalmic Prayer

Many scholars have recognized that there are numerous types of psalms; many of the psalms were used in various special settings such as enthronements and battlefields. There are, however, three main types of psalms found in the biblical prayer book: psalms of well-being/orientation, psalms of lament/disorientation, and psalms of thanksgiving/new orientation (Brueggemann 1984). These three types constitute the largest majority of the psalms. Let's look briefly at each.

Psalms of Well-Being/Orientation

There are in life "seasons of well-being" that call for a prayer that gives voice to the joy, delight, and goodness of God's creation (Brueggemann 1984:19). A good example is Psalm 1, which says essentially that the good will flourish and the wicked will wither. These types of prayers are not concerned that sometimes "bad things happen to good people." This is not to say that these prayers are naive; rather, their focus is to maintain the vision of God's kingdom, to reassure the community that, despite appearances to the contrary, God sits enthroned over a reign of peace. These psalms say, "Relax, God is in control, and God is not worried."

Psalms of Lament/Disorientation

Orientation is well and good, but of the 150 psalms in the Bible, the greatest in number (about one-third) are the laments, the psalms of disorientation, the cries for help. Most Christians are unaware of the full range of emotion that is expressed in the psalms, especially the psalms of lament, and have thereby limited themselves to a narrow range of "acceptable" prayer. The truth is that the psalms complain and moan, rage and roar, question and accuse, and in turn give us great freedom to express the full range of human emotion to our God. There is an earthy spirituality to the psalmist giving full vent to deep hurts and frustrations, waving an angry fist at a God who seems cold and distant. It is wonderfully comforting to know that our God is not only big enough to accommodate this kind of prayer, but in fact encourages it by including it in the Bible's prayer book.

The basic form of this prayer in the Bible usually includes some or all of the following elements: an address, a lament or complaint about one's situation, a petition, motivation clauses, expressions of confidence or trust, and an offer or vow of praise (Miller, 57). Following an overview of each of these elements is an example of how they might be applied to Psalm 22, which is also the basis for a class handout.

Address

Ever since Moses first asked the Creator's name, people have wondered how to address God. In addition to the name revealed to Moses, Yahweh ("I am who I am" or "I will be who I will be"), the Bible gives us a number of other names:

- Elohim (Creator)

- El Elyon (The Most High or Sovereign)

- The Lord our Righteousness

- The Lord will provide

- The Lord send peace

- The Lord my banner

- The Lord that healeth

- The Lord is There (Arthur, 40)

To this list, the psalms add names and images such as "my rock," "the God of my salvation," "my help," "my strength," "God of my right," "my shield," "my stronghold," and "my fortress" (Miller, 60). The most common address in the psalms of lament, however, is simply "O God" or "O Lord" (for "O Yahweh").

The obvious omission from this list is Jesus' own address of God as "Father." Some scholars believe that Jesus' use of this title in the Lord's Prayer derives in part from the psalms in which God refers to the king as "son" (Juel, 60).

Lament or Complaint

The second move of the prayer that cries to the Lord is the lament or complaint. One of the ways that complaints are most often voiced in biblical prayer is through *questions*. These questions, however, are not always rendered in the polite manner of the middle classes! Instead, they challenge what God is doing or has threatened to do. In short, the questions are "a protest, not a request for information" (Miller, 70-71). A wonderful example of a questioning complaint is Psalm 74, in which the two questions "How long?" and "Why?" are put together for maximum effect.

While our faith does not require us to question, it is comforting to know that our faith *permits* such questions, since they usually cannot be avoided (Miller, 133). "The complaining prayer is always on the edge of distrust," says Miller, "which is why the expressions of confidence play such a major role in the psalm prayers for help. The anger and fear and questions about God can be uttered at the deepest level, but only if they are on the lips of trusting creatures who will not let go of that trust even when the facts of the case call into question . . . the presence of God and God's power to deliver" (156).

Petition

After addressing God and stating the emotion behind the request, the psalmist at last comes to the heart of this type of prayer: asking for what is needed. Biblical petitions cover the full range of the human condition and can include requests for healing, forgiveness, or deliverance. Petitions can ask for help, fair judgment, or instruction and guidance; they can seek blessing, salvation, protection, or God's attention; or they can plead for deliverance from enemies, for grace and mercy, or for vindication (Miller, 87ff.).

In the psalms each one of these prayers for help is unique in that each one has at its root the assumption that God's ears are open to the cries of those in need. No need is too little to be uttered in prayer, no request is too trivial to be brought before God. "No holds are barred, no questions or feelings taboo" (Miller, 133).

Motivation

A prominent feature of psalmic prayers is a recounting of the reasons for God to act, typically called the motive or motivational clause. In a sense much of prayer functions in this fashion. When we pray, we present ourselves to God as trustworthy persons who are acting as God would want. Our situation is laid out, and a case is made as to why the Lord should act (Miller, 114-16).

The motivational dimension of psalmic prayers seems natural enough, but can lead to some disturbing conclusions. Underlying this mode of speech is the hint that if the one praying fails to make a case, God will not respond. We need to avoid any suggestion that prayer is purely a matter of saying the right kinds of words in the right kinds of ways. This is an all-too-common concern of many, even if it is never voiced. Instead, we should hold in balance the twin notions that God may be persuaded and that God will not be coerced. This is the stance of the psalms: they assume that God can be moved, that God can be persuaded, and that God's plans can be changed. "Those several places in the Bible where God relents and does not do what God had planned," suggests Miller, "are regularly in response to prayer and the human insistence that there are reasons why God should act to help" (126).

Expressions of Confidence and Trust

The psalms give us freedom to question God and permission to ask for virtually anything concerning the broad range of human need; they also encourage motivational speech to persuade God to act. All of this, however, takes place within a theological understanding that assumes God will be God and will act according to that Divine Nature. In many ways it is a battle of wills, with the psalmist recognizing that God is God, but nonetheless working hard to impress his or her will upon God. "And yet, in another sense," Miller notes, "the prayer for God to act 'according to your steadfast love' or 'for your name's sake' is in the profoundest way possible a call upon God to help, *because that is God's will"* (126).

Expressions of confidence as a part of psalmic prayer are therefore a way of affirming the expectation that God will respond, and that God's response will be according to God's will because God's will is to show forth steadfast love and mercy. These expressions of confidence and trust fill the prayers of the Bible and usually begin with "but" or "yet," as in "yet will I praise" (see Ps. 22).

Offer or Vow of Praise

In some cases it is difficult to know where the expression of confidence ends and the vow to praise begins, but its role remains the same—a way of reaffirming confidence in God. Often the vow is to move the dialogue of prayer out into the community of faith, a promise to praise God in the sanctuary and before the assembled people. Such a move again challenges the notion of "private prayer" as it is typically construed in our day. While we may pray in private, we are called to praise and worship in public so that the redeemed of the Lord may hear and be glad, and so that those who still wait for God's response may take hope.

Psalm 22: A Case Study

A classic example of a prayer of lament is Psalm 22. The parts of the psalm are not laid out in linear fashion, but instead ebb and flow according to the needs of the psalmist. More true to the actual practice of prayer than to some artificial construct of scholarship, the psalms of lament refuse to march in order from address through to a vow to praise. Instead, they cycle around and through, from complaint to trust, from petition to motivation, from praise back to complaint, wherever the needs of the prayer and the emotions of the petitioner lead. This may be important to point out to the class, since many people's reluctance to pray aloud may come from feeling that they can't be as well-ordered as they somehow believe a formal prayer should be. The psalms give permission for "prayers from the heart," words that tumble out until all is said that needs to be said.

Psalm 22: The Prayer of Jesus

My God, my God,　　　　　　　　　　　　　　　ADDRESS
　　why have you forsaken me?　　　　　　　　COMPLAINT
　　Why are you so far from helping me,
　　　　from the words of my groaning?
O my God, I cry by day, but you do not answer;
　　and by night, but find no rest.

Yet you are holy,
　　enthroned on the praises of Israel.　　　　MOTIVATION
In you our ancestors trusted;
　　they trusted, and you delivered them.
To you they cried, and were saved;
　　in you they trusted, and were not put to
　　　　shame.

But I am a worm, and not human;　　　　　　COMPLAINT
　　scorned by others, and despised by the people.
All who see me mock at me;
　　they make mouths at me, they shake their
　　　　heads;
"Commit your cause to the LORD; let him deliver—
　　let him rescue the one in whom he delights!"

Yet it was you who took me from the womb;　　TRUST
　　you kept me safe on my mother's breast.
On you I was cast from my birth,
　　and since my mother bore me
　　you have been my God.
Do not be far from me,　　　　　　　　　　　PETITION
　　for trouble is near
　　and there is no one to help.

Many bulls encircle me, strong bulls of Bashan
　　　　surround me;　　　　　　　　　　　　COMPLAINT
they open wide their mouths at me,
　　like a ravening and roaring lion.

I am poured out like water,
　　and all my bones are out of joint;

my heart is like wax;
    it is melted within my breast;
my mouth is dried up like a potsherd,
    and my tongue sticks to my jaws;
you lay me in the dust of death.

For dogs are all around me;
    a company ofevildoers encircles me.
My hands and feet have shriveled;
    I can count all my bones.
They stare and gloat over me;
    they divide my clothes among themselves,
    and for my clothing they cast lots.

But you, O LORD, do not be far away!   PETITION
    O my help, come quickly to my aid!
Deliver my soul from the sword,
    my life from the power of the dog!
    Save me from the mouth of the lion!

From the horns of the wild oxen
    you have rescued me.
I will tell of your name to my   VOW TO
    brothers and sisters;   PRAISE
    in the midst of the congregation I will praise you:
You who fear the LORD, praise him!
    All you offspring of Jacob, glorify him;
    stand in awe of him, all you offspring of Israel!
For he did not despise or abhor
    the affliction of the afflicted;
he did not hide his face from me,
    but heard when I cried to him.

From you comes my praise in the great congregation;
    my vows I will pay before those who fear him.
The poor shall eat and be satisfied;
    those who seek him shall praise the LORD.
    May your hearts live forever!

All the ends of the earth shall remember
    and turn to the LORD;
    and all the families of the nations
      shall worship before him.
For dominion belongs to the LORD,   PRAISE
    and he rules over the nations.

To him, indeed, shall all who sleep in the
      earth bow down;
    before him shall bow all who go down to
      the dust,
    and I shall live for him.
Posterity will serve him;
    future generations will be told about the Lord,
    and proclaim his deliverance to a people
      yet unborn,
    saying that he has done it.

Psalms of Thanksgiving/Reorientation

At some point, perhaps after a period of lament and disorientation, it comes time to sing a song of thanksgiving and reorientation. These are the new songs, the shouts of joy: God has
responded to the psalmist's cries for help, and so the psalmist
responds in turn with a prayer of thanksgiving.

It is sometimes hard, and probably not necessary or productive, to try to separate praise and thanksgiving in biblical prayer.
They have a shared prompting and often tend to merge into one
another. It is for this reason that "Adoring," as part of the
PRAYER pattern we are teaching in this study, includes adoration, thanksgiving, and praise as similar parts of one movement
in prayer.

The psalms of thanksgiving and reorientation, like the psalms of
lament and disorientation, typically share a common structure. A
prayer of thanksgiving will generally have at least three of these
four movements: expressions and declarations of praise and
thanksgiving, a tendency to show a close connection to the prayer
for help, an announcement to other persons in the community of
God's deliverance, and a communal act of worship, usually a sac-

rifice (Miller, 184). We noted that the vow to praise found in many of the psalms of lament had a stated aim of public praise. As the list above indicates, the community plays a significant part in the prayers of thanksgiving as well. Even if the prayer for help is spoken internally, the psalms are clear that prayers of thanksgiving are spoken long and loud in the presence of the community. "The one who was outside the circle," notes Miller, "now stands at its center but only as the community has become a circle of thanksgiving to God. If human frailty, wickedness, and neglect have contributed to the isolation, it is divine goodness, love, and help that have created the new community of praise and worship" (195).

For Crying Out Loud

The last feature of psalmic prayers that needs to be discussed is their orality. It seems clear that many of the psalms were used in public worship, and several seem especially well-suited to be used responsively, antiphonally, or as bidding prayers. We have noted that the thanksgiving elements of the laments, and the psalms of thanksgiving in their entirety, were spoken out loud in the gathered community. But there is also some evidence that even private prayers were "voiced" prayers. There is in the psalms the recurrent phrase, "I cry to you with my voice." The suggestion seems to be that even in private devotions, prayer is most fully prayer when it is spoken out loud (Mays, 41).

One of the goals for this study is to give participants a level of comfort with praying out loud. We have begun in fairly nonthreatening ways with our printed prayers, and we will continue to be considerate of people's level of comfort as we move ahead. Not everyone will be willing to lead a group prayer at the end of this class (some people are so shy, they won't even lead a silent prayer!), but that's not entirely the point. As the list below shows, there are some significant theological and practical reasons why all of us should pray aloud, even in our private devotions. The orality of the psalms thus opens the door to this discussion, and the suggestion that class members practice psalming out loud until the next class will encourage their vocalization of prayer and break down some of the awkwardness we all feel at hearing ourselves pray.

Here are a few reasons to pray out loud. Feel free to add your own!

- Praying out loud reinforces what we're praying, almost as an echo of our thoughts.
- Praying out loud heightens belief in an Other who is independent from us.
- Praying out loud underscores the nature of prayer as a conversation.
- Praying out loud helps us better understand that when we are silent, we are listening.
- Praying out loud helps us to focus as our thoughts are put into words.
- Praying out loud can help overcome rigid emotional control, allowing greater honesty and freedom in our prayer as speech to God.
- Praying out loud helps cross the threshold between thought and direct address (Mays, 41).
- Praying out loud can lead to greater facility in group praying.

In this conversation someone may raise the issue of the Holy Spirit helping us in our weakness by interceding with "sighs too deep for words" (Rom. 8:26). Certainly there are times, especially when we are in the pit of despair, when sighing and groaning is the only way we can pray (on groaning, see Ps. 22:1; Exod. 2:23-25; Judg. 2:18; Rom. 8:22-23). Yet even these sounds are articulated and remind us of the points noted above.

Teaching the Class

The goals of this class are to build a bridge from the Lord's Prayer to the psalms; to overview the three main types of psalms, paying particular attention to the psalms of lament; and to make a case for the place of spoken prayer, even during our personal devotions.

❖ **Begin the class by leading a responsive prayer based on the interplay between the Lord's Prayer and the psalms** (see "Opening Litany" handout) *(3-5 minutes)*.

Besides building a bridge from last session, this prayer will underscore the fact that the psalms were part of Jesus' own practice and teaching on prayer.

❖ **Lead a discussion on the psalms, including the following elements** *(5-10 minutes)*.

Consider participants' own history with devotional use of psalms:

♦ What successes or frustrations have they had with the psalms as an aid to prayer?

♦ What are the participants' favorite psalms?

If so desired, touch briefly on the psalms in worship in your tradition (i.e., as corporate prayers, in hymnody, etc.). Begin checking the awareness of participants concerning the various types of psalms.

❖ **Move the discussion to a brief lecture/overview of the three types of psalms covered in the chapter** *(15-20 minutes)*.

Since many Christians are unaware of the psalms of lament, the majority of time might be well-spent in that area. The handout entitled "Psalm 22: The Prayer of Jesus" will allow the participants to see how a lament works.

Fill in the worksheet, discussing each of the six parts. Note that

72

phrases beginning with "yet" and "but" are signals in the laments that a change is coming.

Note the nonlinear nature of the six movements, which suggests that prayer is usually more jumbled than what we hear in formal settings (see discussion of Ps. 22).

Underscore the emotional freedom granted by the laments.

❖ **Look for an opportunity to turn the conversation to the oral or "out loud" nature of psalmic prayer** *(10-15 minutes).*

Point out that the corporate use of the psalms suggests that they were prayed aloud. It could also be noted that Jesus' use of Psalm 22:1 from the cross was out loud—and of course reminded those around him about the rest of the psalm that he did not have strength to say, such as the parts in which the psalmist is being mocked and lots are cast for his clothes. Distribute the worksheet entitled "Why Pray Out Loud?" and have participants think of reasons why the biblical pattern of prayer seems to encourage oral prayer. Feel free to supply ideas from the list above as needed. Discuss each idea and have participants make a record on the worksheet.

❖ **Close the class by distributing the handout entitled "'User-Friendly' Psalms," noting especially the suggested assignment** *(5-10 minutes).*

Ask each participant to choose one line from one psalm—either from the list or from a psalm he or she already knows and likes. With the participants bowing in prayer, go around the room and ask each person to read aloud the line chosen as a part of the closing prayer.

❖ **At Home This Week**

Ask participants to continue to use this list of psalms until the next class session, and to pray one psalm *aloud* each day. Encourage participants to consider writing their own psalms in a prayer journal.

Opening Litany

Leader: *Our Father which art in heaven, hallowed be thy name.*

People: The LORD is in his holy temple; the Lord's throne is in heaven. His eyes behold, his gaze examines humankind. Ascribe to the LORD the glory of his name; worship the LORD in holy splendor. (Ps. 11:4; 29:2)

Leader: *Thy kingdom come.*

People: All your works shall give thanks to you, O LORD, and all your faithful shall bless you. They shall speak of the glory of your kingdom, and tell of your power, to make known to all people your mighty deeds, and the glorious splendor of your kingdom. Your kingdom is an everlasting kingdom, and your dominion endures throughout all generations. The LORD is faithful in all his words, and gracious in all his deeds. (Ps. 145:10-13)

Leader: *Thy will be done in earth, as it is in heaven.*

People: Teach me to do your will, for you are my God. Let your good spirit lead me on a level path. (Ps. 143:10)

Leader: *Give us this day our daily bread.*

People: You cause the grass to grow for the cattle, and plants for people to use, to bring forth food from the earth, and wine to gladden the human heart, oil to make the face shine, and bread to strengthen the human heart. (Ps. 104:14-15)

Leader: *And forgive us our debts, as we forgive our debtors.*

People: Have mercy on me, O God, according to your steadfast love; according to your abundant mercy blot out my transgressions. Wash me thoroughly from my iniquity, and cleanse me from my sin. (Ps. 51:1-2)

Leader: *And lead us not into temptation, but deliver us from evil.*

People: You who live in the shelter of the Most High, who abide in the shadow of the Almighty, will say to the LORD, "My refuge and my fortress; my God, in whom I trust." For he will deliver you from the snare of the fowler and from the deadly pestilence; he will cover you with his pinions, and under his wings you will find refuge; his faithfulness is a shield and buckler. (Ps. 91:1-4)

Leader: *For thine is the kingdom, and the power, and the glory, for ever.*

People: Let everything that breathes praise the LORD! Praise the LORD! (Ps. 150:6)

Psalm 22: The Prayer of Jesus

My God, my God,   1 _____
   why have you forsaken me?   2 _____
   Why are you so far from helping me,
      from the words of my groaning?
O my God, I cry by day, but you
      do not answer;
   and by night, but find no rest.
Yet you are holy,
      enthroned on the praisesof Israel.   3 _____
In you our ancestors trusted;
   they trusted, and you delivered them.
To you they cried, and were saved;
   in you they trusted, and were not put to
      shame.
But I am a worm, and not human;   4 _____
   scorned by others, and despised by the
      people.
All who see me mock at me;
   they make mouths at me, they shake their
      heads;
"Commit your cause to the LORD; let him deliver—
   let him rescue the one in whom he delights!"
Yet it was you who took me from the womb;   5 _____
   you kept me safe on my mother's breast.
On you I was cast from my birth,
   and since my mother bore me
   you have been my God.
Do not be far from me,   6 _____
   for trouble is near
   and there is no one to help.
Many bulls encircle me, strong bulls of Bashan
      surround me;   7 _____
   they open wide their mouths at me, like a
      ravening and roaring lion.

I am poured out like water, and all my
    bones are out of joint;
  my heart is like wax; it is melted within
    my breast;
  my mouth is dried up like a potsherd,
    and my tongue sticks to my jaws;
  you lay me in the dust of death.
For dogs are all around me; a company of
    evildoers encircles me.
My hands and feet have shriveled;
    I can count all my bones.
They stare and gloat over me;
  they divide my clothes among themselves,
    and for my clothing they cast lots.
But you, O Lord, do not be far away!   8 _____
  O my help, come quickly to my aid!
Deliver my soul from the sword,
    my life from the power of the dog!
  Save me from the mouth of the lion!
From the horns of the wild oxen you have
    rescued me.
I will tell of your name to
    my brothers and sisters;   9 _____
  in the midst of the congregation I will
    praise you:
You who fear the Lord, praise him!
  All you offspring of Jacob, glorify him;
    stand in awe of him, all you offspring of
    Israel!

For he did not despise or abhor
  the affliction of the afflicted;
  he did not hide his face from me, but heard
   when I cried to him.
From you comes my praise in the great
  congregation;
  my vows I will pay before those who fear
   him.
The poor shall eat and be satisfied;
  those who seek him shall praise the LORD.
  May your hearts live forever!
All the ends of the earth shall remember and
  turn to the LORD;
  and all the families of the nations shall
   worship before him.
For dominion belongs to the LORD,   *10* _____
  and he rules over the nations.
To him, indeed, shall all who sleep in the
  earth bow down;
  before him shall bow all who go down
   to the dust,
  and I shall live for him.
Posterity will serve him;
  future generations will be told about the Lord,
and proclaim his deliverance to a people yet unborn,
  saying that he has done it.

Why Pray Out Loud?

❖

❖

❖

❖

❖

❖

❖

❖

"User-Friendly" Psalms

The psalms can be a little overwhelming for first-time psalmers (people who pray the psalms). Psalms that are "happy" are right next to psalms that are "sad." Psalms that seem to be one person praying are followed by psalms that seem to be prayed by a community, and a strange community at that!

Below is a list of psalms, grouped by topic, that can help you get started. Pick at least one each day between now and the next class, and pray it out loud.

Psalms of Well-Being
1, 8, 23, 25, 26, 46, 63, 84, 91, 101, 103, 104, 105, 107, 108, 111, 112, 113, 128, 131, 133, 134, 135, 139, 141

Psalms of Lament
5, 6, 13, 22, 28, 35, 38 (confession), 42, 43, 51 (confession), 54, 57, 69, 70, 71, 77, 86, 88, 90, 102, 109, 120, 130, 140, 142, 143

Psalms of Thanksgiving
9, 40, 66, 92, 95, 96, 98, 100, 116, 117, 124, 138, 145, 146, 148, 149, 150

Chapter Four
Reconciling

Reconciliation is a good biblical word that seems to be roughly interchangeable with what we usually call forgiveness. We could use the word *forgiveness* instead of the word *reconciliation*, but then our acronym for this study would have to be PFAYER.

To be reconciled is to be made right in a relationship, whether with God, with oneself, or with someone else. The centrality of reconciliation for our lives and for our prayers would be hard to overstate: of all the things Jesus could have pointed us to in his remarkably concise prayer, it is forgiveness that comes second only to the petition for daily bread. Further, in Matthew's recounting of the Lord's Prayer, it is *only* this petition for forgiveness on which Jesus makes immediate commentary (Matt. 6:14-15; see also Matt. 18:35).

Reconciliation, or *forgiveness*, has been defined as giving up "the notion of revenge" (Bondi, 93). To phrase the definition this way acknowledges that we do have such a right, but that it is a right which, if satisfied, will stand in the way of reconciliation, not to mention our own health and healing.

But to define forgiveness this way also places the primary focus of forgiveness on our activity, and risks missing the fact that our being forgiven by God and by others has at least an equal chance of being necessary. Perhaps the best way out of this difficulty is simply to watch how we phrase things, and to offer instead a definition of forgiveness that is less personal, something like this: "to forgive is to be set free from another's right of revenge, or to give up that right oneself."

Unfortunately, we have largely lost sight of both how to be forgiven and how to forgive. In his solid and sweeping book *Embodying Forgiveness*, L. Gregory Jones suggests that the church lacks the ability to make a real difference in people's lives because we have accepted shallow notions of forgiveness. The current enthrallment with counseling and other forms of therapy is due to the failure of the Christian community to embody authentic forgiveness (178). Here we remember the unanswered question of postmodernism, "What will we believe in?" Only as the Christian community bears witness to an authentic and costly forgiveness in Jesus Christ will it have something to offer that is worth believing in.

The problem, of course, is that forgiveness is difficult and costly work, sometimes too difficult and costly. Our pains and hurts are unimaginably deep, often reaching back across the years to childhood. Our sins, as well, are unimaginably deep and often more like bad habits than conscious choices. Since being reconciled to either God or our neighbor seems so difficult and costly, an easier and cheaper kind of forgiveness is invented, if only to cope in the short term. But, Jones notes, "Such versions of cheap, 'therapeutic' forgiveness create the illusion of caring about the quality of human relations while simultaneously masking the ways in which people's lives are enmeshed in patterns of destructiveness. Indeed, such versions of forgiveness often exacerbate human destructiveness precisely because their illusions and masking create a moral and political vacuum" (6).

Most discussions of reconciliation are overbalanced toward the forgiveness we struggle to offer to those who have hurt us. No doubt this occurs because our pain is most acute at this point. From our perspective as individuals, 90 percent of the real work of reconciliation is in our being asked to forgive others. But in point of fact there are three other types of reconciling work that, if we are honest, must somehow account for more than the remaining 10 percent of the work of reconciliation! Being forgiven by God, forgiving oneself, and being forgiven by others are all a part of every life. Perhaps part of Jesus' injunction in the Lord's Prayer is to put the percentages a little closer to what is likely true: we need to be forgiven our sin (against God and others) as much as we need to forgive sin against us (by others and by ourselves).

This chapter will look first at the place of reconciliation in prayer—is this really where such an interpersonal activity takes place? Then we will consider each of the four relationships in which reconciliation gets worked out in our lives. Next we will consider the process of forgiveness. Finally, we will consider two biblical stories of forgiveness in preparation for leading the class through an Ignatian encounter with the living Christ.

Reconciliation and Prayer

It appears to be Jesus' idea to lodge a good bit of the work of reconciliation in the context of prayer. This makes sense when asking God to "forgive us our sins." It is against God that we have sinned; it is to God in prayer that we should go seeking forgiveness for sin. In prayer we can ask forgiveness for the things we know about, and even ask to have revealed to us the things that we don't recognize to be sin. All of this is properly understood to take place using the relationship-specific language of prayer because it is with God that we have these dealings.

But Jesus also seems to suggest that dealing with the horizontal dimension of reconciliation has a place in prayer. How can we understand this work? Reason would dictate that we use another type of relationship-specific language—one appropriate to the relationship needing reconciliation—to resolve such horizontal disconnections. When we make the petition "even as we forgive those who sin against us" as part of our prayer, what are we asking God to do? First, we are asking God to remind us that reconciliation is more of a constant in our lives than we might like to believe. Whether we are the ones doing the forgiving or needing forgiveness, chances are that there is a daily need for some kind of work in this arena. By including it in his model prayer, Jesus suggests that reconciliation will be a constant part of our discipleship.

Second, we are asking God to help us with the hard work of reconciliation. It is hard work to be willing to do it, it is hard work to know how to do it, and it is hard work to keep doing it (understanding that reconciliation is more like a process than a one-time event). This is true whether we are the ones needing forgiveness or the ones doing the forgiving.

Third, we are asking God to move us past abstraction to a reconciliation that is as unique and specific as the situation that gave rise to its need. But such a unique and specific response requires of us more innovation and creativity than we can muster, especially since we are limited by our pain. Indeed, the more severe the offense against us, the more difficult it usually is for us to be innovative in our forgiving. In prayer we ask God to infuse us with innovation and creativity, that we might find a way past our pain and on toward forgiveness.

Prayer might be called a "practice arena of reconciliation." In prayer we are inspired by the Spirit to imagine different scenarios of reconciliation (this may be the offset to our having earlier imagined various scenarios of revenge!). Such imagining can be extremely powerful. In terms of our own reconciliation, an encounter with the risen Christ can be the beginning of a real appropriation of what it means to be forgiven and reconciled to God. In terms of our being reconciled to others, such imagining can be the beginning of freedom and healing. One woman, a victim of sexual abuse by several men, spent many months in counseling talking over her angers and lingering fears. In the course of time she reached a point with each one in which it was time to "take him to the cross." This she would do in prayerful imagination, giving each man to Jesus for either mercy or vengeance. Why? Because both mercy and vengeance belong to the Lord. When we forgive, we give up our lawful right to revenge and let Jesus deal with the person. In the practice arena of prayer we can even ask the Spirit to let us see what Jesus does to the person we give to him. Sometimes we may be surprised!

The Four Relationships of Reconciliation

There are four relationships in which reconciliation gets worked out in our lives. The first of these is our *relationship to God*. Reconciliation with God precedes, and is the foundation for, any other work of forgiveness in our lives. We also need to be *reconciled with ourselves*, and forgiving ourselves is sometimes the most difficult forgiveness. *Being forgiven by others* is often overlooked in discussions of reconciliation, but in any relationship we need to consider that this is at least a possibility. And then finally, but necessarily, we come to the work of *forgiving others their sins against us*. Let's look at each of these in turn.

Reconciliation to God

In his Second Letter to the Corinthians, Paul defines the work of Christ in terms of *reconciliation* and then goes on to talk about a similar work we are to carry out as followers of Christ.

> If anyone is in Christ, there is a new creation: everything old has
> passed away; see, everything has become new! All this is from God,
> who reconciled us to himself through Christ, and has given us the
> ministry of reconciliation; that is, in Christ God was reconciling the
> world to himself, not counting their trespasses against them, and
> entrusting the message of reconciliation to us. So we are ambassa-
> dors for Christ, since God is making his appeal through us; we
> entreat you on behalf of Christ, be reconciled to God. (2 Cor.
> 5:17-20)

In this short statement we come to understand that the work
and message of reconciliation are central to the good news of
Christ. It is a work that is accomplished for us in Christ and a message that we carry forward as we live out that reconciliation with
God and with one another.

What we know about reconciliation, we know because God has
gone before us. God's work on the cross models forgiveness. We
could not live—or forgive—were it not for the reconciling grace
that is central to God's nature and identity. Thus, while the call to
love enemies seems at times huge, Jones suggests that the "paradigm case of refusing to be dominated by hatred, even in the face
of the most severe of betrayals, is none other than that of the
Triune God" (260).

The primacy of God's forgiveness calls for us to reorder our
usual understanding of how the process of forgiveness works.
Many people remain captive to a pre-Christian view of forgiveness.
The scandal of Jesus' preaching was not that he preached forgiveness of sins. The idea of a forgiving God was familiar in first-century
Judaism. But that understanding was predicated on repentance and
on restitution being offered for the wrongs committed. It was only
after such actions that God could be approached and God's forgiveness received (Jones, 108).

Jesus' stunning challenge to this view was the announcement
that God's forgiveness *precedes* repentance. Jesus did not wait for
his outcast friends to repent and become respectable before going
to dinner with them. Instead, "he audaciously burst upon these
sinners with the declaration that their sins had been forgiven, prior
to their repentance, prior to their having done any acts of restitution or reconciliation. *Everything is reversed: you are forgiven;
now you can repent!*" (Wink, 163, emphasis added).

This *a priori* forgiveness is exactly what allows and invites us to repent. Nor does such an offer undermine the importance of repentance. Jesus' preaching makes clear that repentance is still important. But repentance is understood as a response to God's gracious offer of forgiveness. We will return to this priority of forgiveness over repentance when we look at the story of the woman who anointed Jesus, one of many stories in which Jesus pronounced forgiveness of sins without any apparent show of repentance (see Luke 5:17-26, in which Jesus offers forgiveness to a man who was paralyzed; and Luke 19:1-10, in which the offer of forgiveness comes as Jesus goes to Zacchaeus's house to eat with him).

If we have lost sight of how to forgive, perhaps it is because we have lost sight of how to be forgiven. Too many Christians continue to be weighed down by their sin. Unlike the character of Christian in Bunyan's classic *The Pilgrim's Progress*, whose great pack of sin fell from his back and rolled into the empty tomb, people under a great burden fill the pews of the church. We have not yet understood that our sins are forgiven, that we are free to repent and move on. Instead we plod along, a people defeated and in general living lives that don't look that different from the lives of those who are outside the Christian community. No wonder there is no great rush to the church door.

The great good news is that we are forgiven, reconciled to God by the work of Jesus Christ. This work stands before any response we might make, even the response of turning around, of repenting. Forgiveness frees us to turn, to respond with thanksgiving, to forgive.

Reconciliation with Ourselves

We live in a "you-can't-get-something-for-nothing" society. The concept of God's freely choosing to forgive goes against deep understandings of what is right. But reconciliation is not logical. As Doris Donnelly notes, "It is only the person who experiences and survives the unreasonableness of life who can understand the unreasonableness of forgiveness. Once that is understood, mystery is born—and forgiveness is, at its heart, a mystery" (11).

Although much of the focus in discussions of reconciliation is on how hard it is to forgive those who have hurt and harmed us, the

hardest part of the mystery of forgiveness may be forgiving ourselves. This is often especially the case with those who have been
walking with Christ the longest. Old sinful habits emerge again
and again; we despair of ever making anything that looks like
progress, and we shake our heads at the thought that God could
forgive us *again*. Forget seventy times seven. We passed that mark
long ago. Repentance seems like a game, and confession a sham.

One reason it may be hard for us to forgive ourselves is that we
know so many more of the details. We are filled with shame and
self-hatred. This can be the case even if we were in every respect a
victim. Children who have been abused, or whose parents
divorced, or who have been otherwise hurt often believe that it was
something they did that caused their pain. It is their fault, they
believe, and they can carry that burden into adulthood; it becomes
a bitter root that they don't fully understand, something that
springs up without warning.

Whether this is the case, or whether ours is an adult sin, something for which we are fully responsible, we must forgive ourselves. Why? Because to fail to do so is to set ourselves above
God. How dare we say to the Lord who has died for our sin,
"Well, that doesn't matter, I've set a higher standard than you."
How unimaginable that we say to the One who prays for us,
groaning with sighs too deep for words, "No, don't waste your
breath. I'm not worth it." God has called us children; God knows
in even more intimate detail than we do the nature of our sin. God
says, "Return to me, and I will forgive." "What then are we to say
about these things? If God is for us, who is against us?" (Rom.
8:31).

Reconciliation by Others

Once we've been reconciled to God and to ourselves, we are in a
better place to seek reconciliation with those we've sinned against.
Most of us, of course, are more in tune with the pain caused by
those who have sinned against us. But in point of fact there is more
mutuality in most of the situations of our lives than we would like
to admit. In his brief but thought-provoking book *The Forgiveness
of Sins*, Charles Williams notes that we too often fail to recognize
our mutual need for forgiveness: "Many reconciliations have

unfortunately broken down because both parties have come prepared to forgive and unprepared to be forgiven" (113).

Jesus makes an interesting point about our responsibilities in this regard. In the Sermon on the Mount, Jesus offers this advice: "So when you are offering your gift at the altar, if you remember that your brother or sister *has something against you*, leave your gift there before the altar and go; first be reconciled to your brother or sister, and then come and offer your gift" (Matt. 5:23-24, emphasis added). The idea seems to be that we cannot hope to offer a proper gift when we need to be forgiven by someone else, regardless of our felt need for such forgiveness!

Whether unintentionally or otherwise, we have likely slighted someone, offended someone, or hurt someone. It has been said that the greatest danger in communication is believing that it has happened. Given the infinite possibilities for miscommunication, a humble stance of readiness to be forgiven by others just makes sense.

Reconciliation with Others

As we saw earlier, Paul's affirmation to the Corinthian church about our reconciliation with God carries with it an invitation to be about the same reconciling work with one another. In other words, the effect of God's primary work of reconciliation is that we are free to follow God's example and forgive others. God's reconciliation with each of us as individuals is a first step in our reconciling with each other, and one we need to keep firmly in mind as an *a priori* reality that takes primacy over everything else that follows. Part of understanding the primacy of God's forgiveness is that God not only forgives us, God—much to our dismay—holds out the same offer of forgiveness to those we are called to forgive. We can view this truth with everything from mild irony (as in the case of feuding family members or office workers) to absolute horror (as in the case of the child molester or rapist).

To forgive someone else is to be set free. Another way to say this is that there is a difference between the forgiveness that we offer and the forgiveness that is asked for. Forgiveness that we offer is offered in the case of unrepentant offenders, usually without their knowledge. In such a case it is not offered as an "easy out" that somehow dismisses the gravity of the offense, but is offered so that we might be set free from the "ossifying effects" of hatred "as a habit" (Jones, 260). Many in the field of the healing of memories attest to the destructive power of holding on to our hurts. Our anger and pain do nothing to our offenders, but they do disable us emotionally, spiritually, and sometimes even physically. Thus it is that when someone asks to be reconciled, we enter into a process that includes the person as well as his or her repentance and acts of restitution. But often we enter into a process of reconciliation of which the offender is unaware so that we can be free to move on in our lives.

The Process of Reconciliation

Reconciliation is more of a craft than a cure, more of a process-in-time than a point-in-time. There are some predictable parts to an act of reconciliation, and these parts may occur in sequence, overlap, or spiral around and get played again in a new key. The parts of reconciliation can be identified in each of the four types of reconciliation—to God, to ourselves, to one another, and with one another—with different emphases depending on the situation.

The four parts of reconciliation are to *Recognize*, *Review*, *Revision*, and *Revisit*. Let's consider each in turn, and how each is worked out in prayer.

Recognize

This first step has to do with acknowledging that there is a need for reconciliation. To Recognize is to pull aside the curtains that hide our anger, our guilt, and our pain, and to admit that there is a problem. Christians sometimes think that such emotions are denied them. This is not the case. Paul's advice is permission-giving and boundary-setting: "Be angry but do not sin; do not let the sun go down on your anger, and do not make room for the devil" (Eph. 4:26). When we Recognize, we are admitting that we are angry—with ourselves for having sinned against God or neighbor, or with our neighbor for having sinned against us.

This first step in the craft of forgiveness includes "truthful judgment about what has happened or is happening, a willingness to acknowledge both the propriety of anger, resentment, or bitterness and a desire to overcome and be freed from" such feelings (Jones, 231). Recognizing is the first step in reconciling because it signals a desire to change the reality that is. Whether we begin the process of reconciliation in response to God's command, or in order to escape our guilt or anger, what is required is the decision to begin.

Recognizing is a willingness to look, and having seen, to make such a decision. In prayer this decision may come as we ask God to show us our hearts. Jesus' inclusion of a petition about forgiveness as a standard part of our praying should be the trigger to give us pause and make us search for a revelation, Recognizing that somehow, somewhere, in some relationship, reconciliation needs to take place.

Review

Reconciliation requires an honest Review of what has happened. There is no worse advice than to "forgive and forget." But a "judgment of grace" allows us to "remember well." The past "needs to be remembered so that a new and renewed future becomes possible" (Jones, 147).

This may be part of what is behind the biblical injunction to confess our sins one to another (James 5:16). In the case of our own sins, such confession (or Review) provides a means of cleansing and humbling. In the case of the sins of others against us, such confession provides not only a means of cleansing and humbling, but also a means of stating our choice to change the situation. Charles Williams notes that forgiving someone else makes us more aware of the same sin in our own lives, thus provoking "a shy humility on the part not only of the pardoned but of the pardoner" (74).

In the case of someone's sin against us, the person with whom we Review does not necessarily have to be the person with whom we need to be reconciled, although this may often be the case. Let God guide in this. If we go to a third person, we are acting on the biblical injunction that we be for one another a priesthood of believers (1 Pet. 2:5, 9).

In prayer this step of Review is typically called confession. Confession is so central to our identity that Luther said, "When I admonish you to confession I am admonishing you to be a

Christian" (Trueblood, 57). Confessing our sins helps us be truthful with ourselves. This is especially true when we confess to one another. Such confession helps us gain perspective and aids in the work of discernment. Confessing to one another also signals our willingness to be part of a covenant community. This being said, however, Jones notes the importance of:

- appropriate venues for confession, since such practice can easily lead to exhibitionism;
- the need for silence and confidentiality; and
- the need not to exclude those who are unwilling to confess, since the hope is that this is a temporary situation as they journey forward. (182ff.)

A unison prayer of confession is one way of meeting all of these concerns, and perhaps one reason that many traditional liturgies include this kind of prayer in the order of worship.

Revision

The rhythm of reconciliation in prayer is listen-speak-listen-speak. We have listened for God to reveal our hearts, we have spoken our Review, and now we again listen for the Revisioning work of the Holy Spirit. It is here that we ask for help to see something other than what we currently see—ourselves as forgiven by God, ourselves as forgiven by ourselves, ourselves as forgiven by someone else, or someone else as forgiven by us. The most powerful visioning is to give the person in question—either ourselves or another—to Jesus and watch to see what Jesus does. Both vengeance and mercy belong to the Lord (Rom. 12:19), and so we bring the individual in question to the foot of the cross and ask Jesus to do what he will.

One of the most offensive things Christians do, according to Jones, is to "proclaim a general and abstract forgiveness without any regard for the complexities of a specific situation or a particular person's life." Every situation is unique and must be handled as such; otherwise, we run the risk of trivializing the suffering, or worse, the *sufferer*. "God's forgiveness is universal in scope," says Jones, "but it cannot be abstract" (228-29).

Prayer is the perfect place for the Holy Spirit to accomplish the needed creative work, inspiring (*in* + *spirare*, to breathe into) the unique response called for by the current need for reconciliation. The creative work of the Spirit shows us how to balance judgment and grace, giving wisdom to find a "judgment of grace." The creative work of the Spirit helps us to remember well "so that we can envision and embody a future different from the past. In that sense, we need the Spirit both to return to us our memories and also to enliven our imaginations" (Jones, 149).

To speak of the Spirit's ability to enliven our imaginations and envision a new future reminds us of the power of language to construe alternative reality.[1] Again, if we take seriously an integral worldview, in which what we say in prayer has an effect on the material world, then we are coming to understand that something *happens* in our prayers for reconciliation. The Spirit breaks into our pain, inspires an alternative and hopeful future vision, and aids us to speak an innovative and wise word that has an instrumental effect in constructing that alternative reality. This is true, again, whether we are the ones needing forgiveness or needing to forgive. In the former case, the Spirit may help us to see that we have injured another and grant us a vision of humility to ask for and receive forgiveness. In the latter case, which for most of us is much harder to imagine, we find the needed strength to forgive our offender, if only to be able to move on with our lives.

Revisit

Again, reconciliation is not so much an event as it is a process. Christians have been misled into believing that if they can't "forgive and forget," that if the old feelings come up again, then they have somehow failed at forgiveness. In contrast, C. S. Lewis writes to Malcolm: "To forgive for the moment is not difficult, but to go on forgiving, to forgive the same offence again every time it recurs to the memory—there's the real tussle" (*Letters to Malcolm*, 29-30, quoted in Jones, 237).

Perhaps this is part of why Jesus suggested to Peter that we are to forgive not seven times, but seventy times seven: it is not necessarily that our offender will sin against us that many times, but that we will likely replay the offense in our memory that many times and more! Thus, every time the old feelings return we Revisit our previous decision and, with the aid of the Holy Spirit, prayerfully speak words of forgiveness and reconciliation once more.

A brief word needs to be said here about reconciliation and "repeat offenders." In many cases the damage wrought on an individual by abuse (particularly in the instance of spouse or child abuse) is only just a little worse than the damage wrought on that same individual by a church that demands that the abused party "forgive" and return to such a situation. Forgiveness does not preclude accountability, and reconciliation does not preclude punishment. A superficial or spiritualized notion of reconciliation that does nothing to present a "grace of judgment" has missed the essence of God's message in Jesus Christ.

An Ignatian Exercise in Forgiving Prayer

Ignatius Loyola founded the Jesuit order in the sixteenth century. One of his contributions to the spiritual development of the community was a method of meditating on scripture. The idea is simple: Ignatius invites us to use the "sensible imagination" to put ourselves into a biblical story—to see who and what is there, to hear the words that are spoken, to smell the smells of sheep and sweat, and to feel the textures of coarse-woven fabrics or a baby's soft skin. While this type of exercise will appeal to certain personality types more than others, almost everyone can benefit from using the imagination to explore a biblical story.

Once we enter into a story through this kind of meditation, it is a short step to turning the meditation to prayer. Overhearing Jesus as he heals a person who is paralyzed or blesses the multitudes, we can present ourselves to him in our mind's eye and thus speak and listen for his word to us in this prayerful attitude. These encounters can be immensely powerful, and the leader is advised to be prepared for a wide range of responses in leading such an exercise as part of this lesson. Although it is sometimes hard for us to believe, the Holy Spirit hovers over all our spiritual activity, waiting for an opportunity to come and change lives. This could happen even in the confines of a class on prayer!

Let's look at two stories ripe with possibility for an Ignatian approach to prayer.

The Woman Who Anointed Jesus

In Luke 7 we find a wonderfully rich story of a woman who vio-
lated custom and convention to anoint Jesus. It is a story of forgiveness that demonstrates, among other things, our contention
that forgiveness precedes repentance and, indeed, invites such
action as response.

One of the Pharisees asked Jesus to eat with him, and he went
into the Pharisee's house and took his place at the table. And a
woman in the city, who was a sinner, having learned that he was
eating in the Pharisee's house, brought an alabaster jar of ointment. She stood behind him at his feet, weeping, and began to
bathe his feet with her tears and to dry them with her hair. Then
she continued kissing his feet and anointing them with the ointment. Now when the Pharisee who had invited him saw it, he
said to himself, "If this man were a prophet, he would have
known who and what kind of woman this is who is touching
him—that she is a sinner." Jesus spoke up and said to him,
"Simon, I have something to say to you." "Teacher," he replied,
"Speak." "A certain creditor had two debtors; one owed five
hundred denarii, and the other fifty. When they could not pay, he
canceled the debts for both of them. Now which of them will
love him more?" Simon answered, "I suppose the one for whom
he canceled the greater debt." And Jesus said to him, "You have
judged rightly." Then turning toward the woman, he said to
Simon, "Do you see this woman? I entered your house; you gave
me no water for my feet, but she has bathed my feet with her
tears and dried them with her hair. You gave me no kiss, but
from the time I came in she has not stopped kissing my feet. You
did not anoint my head with oil, but she has anointed my feet
with ointment. Therefore, I tell you, her sins, which were many,
have been forgiven; hence she has shown great love. But the one
to whom little is forgiven, loves little." Then he said to her,
"Your sins are forgiven." But those who were at the table with
him began to say among themselves, "Who is this who even forgives sins?" And he said to the woman, "Your faith has saved
you; go in peace." (Luke 7:36-50)

The woman has evidently heard Jesus' message of God's grace
and forgiveness (see Luke 5:32). What she does at Simon's dinner
party is a response of love, a sacramental act that marks a new
beginning, a turning around. She has been forgiven; *hence* she is
able to show great love (7:47). A lot hinges on this little word

hence. In Greek it is *hoti* and is often translated as "because" or "for." But to translate it "because" leads us to a belief that Jesus only forgives the sins of those who show proper humility and deference. Jesus tells Simon a story that gives the key: both debtors are forgiven, and their *response* of love is in proportion to their debt. The debt is forgiven; *hence* she is able to show great love.

Once we've made clear the intellectual meaning of the text, we are free to enter into the story itself. It is a story that drips with possibility for the sensible imagination, with the sound of voices over their dinner, the clatter of tableware, and the smell of the food. Then suddenly a woman enters, and conversation stops. We see the astonishment in the eyes of the host and other dinner guests as she cries over Jesus' feet (the posture at meals was to recline with feet curved back from the table). We hear her sobs, see the gleam of the alabaster jar, smell the perfume as it fills the room. Now a new sound as the woman kisses Jesus' feet—and a new sight, horrified looks!

What perspective we take depends on how the Spirit prods. Are we the woman, Simon, one of the dinner guests, or perhaps one of the servants silently clinging to the shadows? From our perspective we then hear the ensuing conversation between Jesus and Simon, and we are left to draw our own conclusions: Do we owe fifty or five hundred? The clear implication, of course, is that even if we didn't owe five hundred, we would want to so that our love could be greater.

The story leaves off where the real work of Spirit-led imagination begins. No matter who we are as we listen to the story, we find a way to talk with Jesus. What is his look, his posture, his expression? What does he say to us? How do we respond? After several minutes of silence, invite participants to journal this prayerful exchange and any insights that come to them.

The Man Who Denied His Master

There is perhaps no more poignant story of forgiveness than that which unfolds on a beach along the Sea of Galilee. Here Jesus reclaims the disciple most of us can relate to—one whose love and denial come through in painful detail.

When they had gone ashore, they saw a charcoal fire there, with fish on it, and bread. Jesus said to them, "Bring some of the fish that you have just caught." So Simon Peter went aboard and hauled the net ashore, full of large fish, a hundred fifty-three of them; and though there were so many, the net was not torn. Jesus said to them, "Come and have breakfast." Now none of the disciples dared to ask him, "Who are you?" because they knew it was the Lord. Jesus came and took the bread and gave it to them, and did the same with the fish. This was now the third time that Jesus appeared to the disciples after he was raised from the dead.

When they had finished breakfast, Jesus said to Simon Peter, "Simon son of John, do you love me more than these?" He said to him, "Yes, Lord; you know that I love you." Jesus said to him, "Feed my lambs." A second time he said to him, "Simon son of John, do you love me?" He said to him, "Yes, Lord; you know that I love you." Jesus said to him, "Tend my sheep." He said to him the third time, "Simon son of John, do you love me?" Peter felt hurt because he said to him the third time, "Do you love me?" And he said to him, "Lord, you know everything; you know that I love you." Jesus said to him, "Feed my sheep." (John 21:9-17)

Here again, it is helpful to gain an intellectual insight into the passage before we plunge in further. As a master storyteller John provides us with all the clues we need to know exactly what is intended. For starters, Jesus has started a charcoal fire. The word used here appears only one other time in John's Gospel, and it is in reference to the fire around which Peter warmed himself in the courtyard of the high priest, "the fire of denial." Then there is the inescapable parallel between Peter's three denials and Jesus' three questions about love. This is not simply a story of forgiveness, but a story of triple forgiveness and a love that burns away a heart's pain.

The sensible imagination might begin its meditation by taking in the sounds and smells of that lonely strip of beach—the gentle lap of the water, the wind as it blows, the cry of a bird. There is a chill in the early morning air, and so the fire feels welcome. But it is an uneasy scene, no matter whose perspective we take, whether that of Peter or one of the other disciples (it is probably best to avoid becoming one of the 153 fish, as tempting as that might be). The most helpful route might be to become one of the other disciples, and to eat our breakfast quietly and thoughtfully as we overhear the exchange between Peter and Jesus. And again, the work of imagination in prayer can begin in earnest where the story ends. After Jesus finishes speaking, as sand is being kicked on the fire and the boats are being made ready for the short trip back down to Capernaum, we quietly edge toward Jesus, our own denials and loves only too ready to be confessed. What does Jesus look like there in the morning sun? Does he frown as we confess our failure, or is there a gleam in his eye? And after we've spilled our guts, does he walk away shaking his head, or are we enveloped in a giant bear hug? What words does he speak, what challenge to feed or to serve does he deliver?

Prayerful Work

Reconciliation is prayerful work. We attend to this work in prayer because it is such constant and hard work. Whether it is our need to be reconciled to God, to another, or with someone who has hurt us, there is almost no end to the task.

There is also almost no end to the pain. The wounds that give rise to the need for reconciliation are sometimes almost beyond imagining—almost. But even if it takes a lifetime, the Spirit gently breathes hope into our weary hearts—hope that we might be forgiven after all, hope that we might forgive after all. This inspiration of hope fires the imagination and helps us to shape prayer that can change lives.

Teaching the Class

The goals of this class are to explore Reconciling as a move of prayer and to experience a prayerful encounter with the risen Christ using the Ignatian method of prayer.

❖ **Greet participants and get feedback on using the psalms in prayer** *(3-5 minutes)*.

❖ **Distribute "A Prayer of Confession" from Psalm 51 to use as the opening prayer** *(2 minutes)*.

❖ **Distribute "An Old-Fashioned Bible Study" worksheet and facilitate its completion** *(20-30 minutes; make sure everyone has a Bible and something to write with)*.

Draw on your reading of the background material for this chapter to help participants understand the four moves of reconciliation and the place of reconciliation in prayer.

❖ **Distribute the worksheet entitled "A Reconciling Encounter with Jesus" and lead an Ignatian meditation on a story of forgiveness** *(15-20 minutes; provide pens)*.

You may want to use one of the two stories reviewed in the chapter. Begin by explaining to participants what they will be asked to do: to use their imaginations to enter into a story as you tell it, and at some point, to continue it on their own in silence. Choose only *one* story to use for this experience.

Read through the story out loud and take a few minutes to unpack its central meaning. Then invite participants to get comfortable. Most will probably want to close their eyes. Describe the scene in as much detail as possible, engaging the senses of sight, sound, smell, and touch. Take your time suggesting these details, pausing for several seconds after mentioning each element to give participants a chance to bring them to life in their imaginations.

Move to a listing of the various people in the scene. As you name them, invite the participants to imagine themselves as one of these characters or to envision someone else they would rather be and take a place in the scene. Pause more often and for longer periods of time (perhaps as much as a minute). The longer the exercise goes, the less important the leader's words become as the Holy Spirit begins to direct the action.

Having set the stage, slowly read through the dialogue in the biblical story. At the conclusion of the written dialogue invite participants to see themselves approaching or being approached by Jesus. What are they prompted to say to him, and how does he respond? Suggest that participants enter into a silent, imagined dialogue with Jesus. Encourage them to take their time, both to hear and speak in their imaginations. As the images fade, invite them to write down the conversation and any insights it prompts.

❖ At Home This Week

Encourage participants to continue praying the psalms and to begin practicing the prayer of Reconciling. Also, suggest that they use the story above that you did not use in class as the basis for an Ignatian encounter at home.

If you have made arrangements for your group to take a personality test, this should also be done at home this week (see introduction for further information).

A Prayer of Confession
Psalm 51:1-12

Leader: *Have mercy on me, O God,*
according to your steadfast love;

People: according to your abundant mercy
blot out my transgressions.

Leader: *Wash me thoroughly from my iniquity,*
and cleanse me from my sin.

People: For I know my transgressions,
and my sin is ever before me.

Leader: *Against you, you alone, have I sinned,*
and done what is evil in your sight,

People: so that you are justified in your sentence
and blameless when you pass judgment.

Leader: *Indeed, I was born guilty,*

People: a sinner when my mother conceived me.

Leader: *You desire truth in the inward being;*

People: therefore teach me wisdom in my secret heart.

Leader: *Purge me with hyssop, and I shall be clean;*

People: wash me, and I shall be whiter than snow.

Leader: *Let me hear joy and gladness;*

People: let the bones that you have crushed rejoice.

Leader: *Hide your face from my sins,*

People: and blot out all my iniquities.

All: Create in me a clean heart, O God,
and put a new and right spirit within me.
Do not cast me away from your presence,
and do not take your holy spirit from me.
Restore to me the joy of your salvation,
and sustain in me a willing spirit.

Reconciling
An Old-Fashioned Bible Study

1. Read Matthew 6:9-15. What is the only petition of the Lord's Prayer upon which Jesus provided commentary?

2. For the purposes of this study "reconciliation" refers to the work of mending relationships torn apart by sin. This work includes forgiveness, repentance, and confession. Reconciliation can take place in four different relationships:

- *Reconciliation to God:* Read 2 Corinthians 5:17-20. What is the central truth about the work of Jesus Christ?

- *Resonciliation to ourselves:* Read Romans 8:31. Why is it that we are often harder on ourselves than even the God who forgives?

- *Reconciliation to others:* Read Matthew 5:23-24. Whose responsibility is it to make things right if someone has something against us?

- *Reconciliation with others:* Read Colossians 3:13. How are we enabled to forgive others?

3. Reconciliation is a more of a craft than a cure, more of a process than an event. Still, there are some predictable parts to an act of reconciliation:

Reveal: Read Ephesians 4:26
Uncover emotions and denials, and own the need for a process of reconciliation to begin

Prayer

Review: Read James 5:16
Confess to at least one other person the details of the situation.

Revision: Read Romans 12:19
Forgiveness is a decision to give up our right to revenge and instead entrust ourselves or our offenders to Jesus. To revision is to ask the Holy Spirit to help us see a new way to be, as we take ourselves and/or our offenders to the foot of the cross and watch as Jesus shows either vengeance or mercy. Sometimes we may be surprised!

Revisit: Read Matthew 18:21-35
Every time old feelings return, forgive (or be forgiven) again!

A Reconciling Encounter
with Jesus

Listen to the story told by the leader. Imagine you are there. Sense all the details. What do you see? What do you hear? Are there tastes and smells and textures?

As the story unfolds, choose a character for yourself. You may choose to be one of the main characters, or you may decide to create a role not readily evident in the scene (there was almost always a crowd around watching Jesus as he interacted with others).

As the story concludes you are invited to continue your own dialogue with Jesus. Do this silently, and in your imagination talk with Jesus and hear what he says to you. After several minutes, as you sense the scene coming to an end, use this page to write down the conversation and any insights you draw from this encounter with your Lord.

Chapter Five

Adoring

A disservice done to people in the pew—sometimes intentional-ly, sometimes unintentionally—is the suggestion of a "one size fits all" spirituality. Over the centuries, many prayer resources of the church have been developed by people whose temperament type tends to put them into leadership, but whose style of prayer differs from almost 90 percent of the larger population (Michael and Norrisey, 79). Whether implicitly or explicitly, church members are encouraged to pattern their prayers and spiritual practices on those of the clergy, even if they are of a different spiritual temperament. The problem is further exaggerated by different preferences concerning styles of spirituality, different stages of psychosocial growth, different faith and moral stages, and even different generational backgrounds.

This chapter briefly surveys two of these areas—*temperament indicators* and *styles of spirituality*—that affect an individual's practice of prayer. The hope is that this will help free class participants to explore their particular set of circumstances and to find greater latitude in their prayer lives. It is particularly fitting that this conversation should take place as a background for our third prayer movement of Adoring, since this area holds tremendous promise for diverse expressions of praise to God.

Temperament Indicators for Spirituality

In *Prayer and Temperament: Different Prayer Forms for Different Personality Types*, authors Chester P. Michael and Marie C. Norrisey set out the results of the Prayer Project, conducted in 1982. More than four hundred people engaged in a year-long study to determine the value of using various prayer forms according to sixteen different personality types as determined by the Myers-Briggs Type Indicator (MBTI).

The study was a great success, and the book is well worth reading. It contains information on the MBTI and subsequent research by Isabel Myers and by David Kiersey. Seeking to follow the quite ancient tradition that there are essentially four basic temperaments, Kiersey has suggested four key pairings that have to do with external behavior. These four pairings he lists (using the MBTI system) as Intuition-Thinking (NT), Sensing-Judging (SJ), Intuition-Feeling (NF), and Sensing-Perceiving (SP). In his work Kiersey cites four Greek gods as representatives of these four temperaments, which he labels Promethean (NT), Epimethean (SJ), Apollonian (NF), and Dionysian (SP). These are roughly equivalent to those proposed by Hippocrates in the fifth century: phlegmatic (NT), melancholic (SJ), choleric (NF), and sanguine (SP) (Michael and Norrisey, 15-16). Some people in the class will recognize this basic idea, if not exactly these terms, from business and management training courses (for example, one uses animals—dolphins, bulls, bears, and monkeys—to designate the four temperament types!).

Being good Catholics, Michael and Norrisey have chosen to use four fathers of the faith as representatives of the four basic types. What follows is an overview of their four types, referred to as Thomistic (NT), Ignatian (SJ), Augustinian (NF), and Franciscan (SP).

Thomistic Prayer (NT)

Characteristics of the Thomistic Temperament: logical; enjoys mental challenges; tends to rearrange environment (organizers); leaders; perfectionists; critical; demanding; likely to schedule even play time; communication tends to be precise, with a reluctance to state the obvious; straightforward; future oriented; desire for competency (Michael and Norrisey, 80-81).

"The type of prayer most suitable to this temperament is the logical, rational, discursive meditation whereby the intellect leads one from one proposition to another until a logical conclusion is drawn in the form of some resolution or ethical demand" (Michael and Norrisey, 82-83). Malcolm Goldsmith, in his worthwhile book *Knowing Me, Knowing God*, adds, "Thinking prayer is often full of doubts and points of view. . . . It can be highly self-critical and deprecating, but also can be effective, well thought through, consistent, and to the point." Goldsmith suggests that thinkers "tend to regard themselves as rather inadequate" in matters of prayer (79).

But the Thomistic temperament might fruitfully show adoration by studying it from every possible angle, probably using the seven auxiliary questions: *what, why, how, who, where, when, with what helps* (Michael and Norrisey, 83). Prayer might then meditate along the lines of: What do we mean by adoration? Why should I adore God? How can I best show my adoration to God? Who are some of the people in the Bible or in history who can give examples of adoration? When and where can I best show God my adoration? What aids can I use to help me in my adoration of God? (Michael and Norrisey, 83).

Ignatian Prayer (SJ)

Characteristics of the Ignatian Temperament: wants to feel useful; typical of givers rather than receivers; practical; work ethic; strong sense of tradition; conscientious; can be pessimistic—"If I don't do it, who will?"; tends to enjoy ceremony and ritual; typical of great law and order people; careful; cautious; accurate; industrious; and always prepared (Michael and Norrisey, 47-48). Michael and Norrisey note that 50 percent of the congregation on an average Sunday will be Ignatians, and so it is worthwhile for clergy (who are less likely to be of this type) to offer prayer forms that speak to this segment of the population (48).

"The purpose of Ignatian prayer is to try to make the Gospels and the Scripture scenes become so alive and real to us that we can make a personal application of the teaching or message contained therein." As we enter into biblical stories, "Ignatius suggests that we try to use all five senses during our imaginary journey back to the events of salvation history" (see chapter 4). Ignatian prayer tries to imagine "not only what we would see but also what each of the characters involved would say," what the physical objects would feel like, and what smells and tastes might be part of the experience (Michael and Norrisey, 50).

So, for example, the Ignatian might show adoration by using the "sensible imagination" to journey back into some of the key stories in the Bible, identifying with one or more of the original participants and giving praise and thanks to God at the conclusion of the journey for the salvation God has wrought. The joy of Miriam at the crossing of the Red Sea (Exod. 15:21), Hannah at the birth of Samuel (1 Sam. 2), and Mary at the conception of Jesus (Luke 1), or the celebration of Joseph on being reunited with his brothers (Gen. 45), King David at the return of the Ark to Israel (2 Sam. 6), or even John in his great vision of the new Jerusalem (Rev. 21)—each of these stories might make a fruitful prayer meditation of adoration for the Ignatian temperament.

Augustinian Prayer (NF)

Characteristics of the Augustinian Temperament: usually creative; optimistic; verbal; persuasive; outspoken; great need for self-expression; tends to communicate with others easily; typical of good listeners; hates conflict; prefers face-to-face encounters; deep feelings; highly committed to helping others; compassionate; enthusiastic; always searching for meaning, authenticity, and self-identity; natural rescuers (Michael and Norrisey, 59-60).

The person who prays this type of prayer is "never content with the superficial, external meaning of a Scripture passage"; there is always a quest to discover "What message is the Lord trying to convey to me in this story?" "A spiritual journal, where thoughts and inspirations are recorded, is a great help" in this kind of prayer. Augustinians often feel that they can best pray "at the point of a pen" (Michael and Norrisey, 62-63).

So, for example, an Augustinian showing adoration might do so in a written dialogue of praise and thanksgiving. The last five psalms (146-150) could well be used by substituting the Augustinian's own name or person for any pronoun or personal reference.

Franciscan Prayer (SP)

Characteristics of the Franciscan Temperament: free; unconfined; impulsive; dislikes being tied down by rules; loves action; easily bored with the status quo; crisis-oriented; good troubleshooters; flexible; open-minded; adaptable; willing to change position; tends to live very much in the present; dislikes practice and prefers to "just do it" (Michael and Norrisey, 69-70).

Since it is easy for Franciscan types to "see God in the whole of creation, they are able to make a fruitful meditation on the beauty of a flower, a meadow, a lake, a waterfall, a mountain, the ocean, or any event of nature" such as a sunrise, a sunset, or a change of the season. Sometimes a musical instrument, a paintbrush, dancing, or "anything that involves movement, action, and the senses" can be a prayerful way for Franciscans to show forth love for God (Michael and Norrisey, 71-73).

So, for example, the Franciscan showing adoration in prayer might do very well with a musical instrument, craft project, liturgical dance, or any other expression that involves the five senses. A walk through the woods in which one pauses to give thanks and praise for all that is seen would also be a fitting prayer for the Franciscan temperament (Michael and Norrisey, 73).

Just for Fun

Someone, somewhere, put together one-sentence prayers for each of the sixteen temperament types and floated them on the Internet. Here's what the person wrote. Enjoy!

ISTJ: Lord, help me to relax about insignificant details, beginning tomorrow at 11:41:23 A.M. (EST).

ISTP: God, help me to consider people's feelings, even if most of them ARE hypersensitive.

ESTP: God, help me to take responsibility for my own actions, even though they're usually NOT my fault.

ESTJ: God, help me to try not to RUN everything. But, if You need some help, just ask.

ISFJ: Lord, help me to be more laid-back and help me to do it EXACTLY right.

ISFP: Lord, help me to stand up for my rights (if you don't mind my asking).

ESFP: God, help me to take things more seriously, especially parties and dancing.

ESFJ: God, give me patience, and I mean right NOW!

INFJ: Lord, help me not be a perfectionist. (Did I spell that correctly?)

INFP: God, help me to finish everything I sta

ENFP: God, help me to keep my mind on one th—Look a bird—ing at a time.

ENFJ: God, help me to do only what I can and trust you for the rest. Do you mind putting that in writing?

INTJ: Lord, keep me open to others' ideas, WRONG though they may be.

INTP: Lord, help me be less independent, but let me do it my way.

ENTP: Lord, help me follow established procedures today. On second thought, I'll settle for a few minutes.

ENTJ: Lord, help me slow downandnotrushthroughwhatIdo.

Styles of Spirituality

Another seminal thinker in the area of spiritual types and forms is Ben C. Johnson. In his book *Pastoral Spirituality* he lays out several styles of spirituality and prayer that people have historically used to show devotion to God.

Evangelical Spirituality

According to Johnson, evangelical spirituality is centered on an encounter with God through the Word of God. Reading and understanding scripture and seeking and doing the will of God are Christ-centered means of a vital spirituality. As might be assumed from its name, evangelical spirituality is highly interested in personal witness to others with an aim toward conversion. Clear guidelines for living are generally presented and include a strong emphasis on a daily time for reading the Bible and for prayer. Johnson suggests that evangelical spirituality has a strong appeal to the sensate (SJ [Ignatian] or SP [Franciscan]) type of personality and may also attract more extroverts than introverts.

Summarizing its strengths, Johnson suggests that this form of spirituality creates a passionate, committed, sacrificial, and hard-working person. Its weaknesses might be a tendency toward legalism and judgmentalism (1988:68-69).

A prayer of adoration offered out of evangelical spirituality might be filled with biblical ascriptions of praise and thanksgiving. The focus of such adoration would perhaps be "God's mighty acts" in bringing salvation to people of all times and places. Evangelical adoration would be sure to include thanksgiving for all of God's previous answers to prayer and would perhaps even have a prayer list against which to check prior requests and their answers. Such prayer would likely be offered in boldness and in the assurance that God would be pleased to hear it.

Charismatic Spirituality

The focus of charismatic spirituality is on the immediate presence of God through the work of the Holy Spirit. This experience is found primarily in worship and praise services, but also in Bible study and small group sharing. There is a freedom in worship and expression that flows from a focus on the gifts of the Spirit. The raising of hands, the use of liturgical movement, and a freer musical style are often found in worship that flows from the basis of charismatic spirituality. This spirituality is also generally more willing to express emotion as God is encountered. Johnson suggests that charismatic spirituality often appeals to an intuitive type of person (NF [Augustinian]) who feels devotion to Christ. He further suggests that many of this type will tend to be extroverts, and thus more comfortable than introverts in expressing this emotional attachment to their Lord (70).

Summarizing its strengths, Johnson notes that the focus on the immediate experience of God usually leads to a high level of dedication and sacrifice; further, he says, this form of spirituality is well able to cross racial and socioeconomic boundaries. Weaknesses stem from two overemphases: first, on emotion, sometimes to the neglect of intellectual process, and second, on personal experience, sometimes to the neglect of concern for social transformation (70).

A prayer of adoration offered out of charismatic spirituality might also be filled with biblical ascriptions of praise and thanksgiving like that of its cousin, evangelical spirituality. The many names of God, likely offered in their original Hebrew, might provide a way of remembering the many ways in which God has been at work in one's life. Charismatic adoration would probably include singing and/or listening to praise-type music, and might include the lifting of hands in a gesture of _todah_ (the Hebrew word for thanksgiving that suggests an action as well as an attitude).

Sacramental Spirituality

In sacramental spirituality the experience of God is known through the sacraments—primarily the Lord's Supper—and through the whole of the worship service. Liturgical prayers, usually more formal in nature, and the changing seasons of the liturgical year are part of what helps frame this type of spirituality. In contrast to some aspects of charismatic spirituality, sacramental spirituality offers structure and shape through the use of a prayer book, a hymnbook, and other traditional worship aids. Johnson suggests that this type of spirituality might appeal more to the sensate, thinking (NT [Thomistic]) type of personality (71).

The strength of this spirituality is its objectivity: no matter how we feel, no matter the depth or authenticity of our personal faith, the sacraments are real and effective. On the other hand, the weakness may be a "dependence upon ritual that can become empty" (71).

A prayer of adoration offered from the perspective of sacramental spirituality might draw on the great liturgical tradition of the church. Indeed, the Book of Common Prayer offers many such prayers of thanksgiving, and the sacrament itself centers, in part, on the "Great Thanksgiving," a prayer that rehearses the sacred history. A prayer such as this, far from being wooden and rigid, is offered out of reverence for tradition and as a testimony to the validity of carefully worded prayers that thoughtfully glorify God.

Activist Spirituality

This type of spirituality, Johnson suggests, is most often found in the left wing of mainline churches and in religious groups that gather around specific issues (such as peace, ecology, and feminism). The focus for this type of spirituality is not in worship so much as it is in action. God is met as one serves in society and is politically active. For the activist, the kingdom of God is not "pie-in-the-sky by-and-by," but can be glimpsed here and now as we become the hands, feet, and voice of our living Lord. This kind of spirituality may attract an extroverted, intuitive, feeling type of personality (NF [Augustinian]) (71).

The strength of this type of spirituality lies in its high ideals and intention to make a difference in the world. Its weakness, perhaps predictably, lies in a tendency to lose awareness of God while focusing on activity in the world; thus stripped of spiritual motivation, discouragement is not far behind (72).

The prayer of adoration offered by the activist would clearly be the action itself. The sense of satisfaction, accomplishment, or peace that follows from a good act done in godly affection would be counted a sufficient prayer. In this vein, the corporate nature of activist spirituality might show itself as the group relived the moment and shared together a sense of thanksgiving and praise.

Academic Spirituality

While perhaps not readily discernible as a form of spirituality, there is, historically, a group of people who have sought to know and experience God through thinking, reading, and research. For the academic, God is encountered through rational thought, study, analysis, and reflection, and that encounter is then expressed in writing and teaching. Academic spirituality is probably most attractive to an introverted, intuitive type of personality (NT [Thomistic]), and may be strongly represented by, but not necessarily limited to, those who are professional teachers, scholars, theologians, and more academically minded clergy (72).

The strengths of this spirituality include a search for truth and a willingness to face issues honestly and without sentimentalism or emotionalism. Its weaknesses can include a loss of respect for the holy and a tendency toward cynicism (72).

The prayer of adoration offered out of academic spirituality might draw on both the activist's sense of accomplishment and the sacramentalist's love of careful words well ordered. The prayer would likely show great forethought and would certainly reflect the fruit of the academic's scholarship. Although the prayer might not be written, it would not be unusual for the academic to pray a prayer of adoration by writing it down, perhaps even as a work of poetry.

Ascetic Spirituality

Less understandable to many in mainstream contemporary culture, ascetic spirituality is often found in monastic orders and has a Protestant parallel in "world-denying holiness movements." "The ascetic," says Johnson, "lives a life of contemplation and self-denial as an expression of devotion to God" (73). A simple life of prayer, rest, and work defines this form of spirituality, as well as vows of poverty, chastity, and obedience. This type of spirituality, Johnson suggests, will appeal to introverted, sensate types of personalities (SJ [Ignatian] or SP [Franciscan]) (73).

The clear strengths of this type of spirituality come from its strong sense of discipline, humility, and in most cases, Christian community. The clear weaknesses are the temptation toward escapism, a rigid discipleship that can in time become empty, and a tendency toward works-righteousness (73).

The prayer of adoration most comfortable for the ascetic, like that of the sacramentalist, would likely draw on the great traditions of the church. But perhaps more than any other, the ascetic might be best able to see all of life as a prayer, whether liturgical or lived. The rhythm of work and worship observed by ascetic communities is, in fact, designed to make just this point. Thus, the ascetic may make eating a bowl of oatmeal an act of thanksgiving, the simple joy of taking time to notice texture and taste a conscious act of adoration to the Giver of all good gifts.

Overlaying Temperament and Spirituality Types

It is probable that each person, upon reading these various descriptions, will have little difficulty identifying where he or she feels the most comfortable. The rich and complex mix of genes, family background, experience, and socialization that produces personality, together with the particular form of spirituality to which we've become most accustomed, can be used to locate our usual form of prayer on a matrix like the one below.

HISTORICAL FORMS OF SPIRITUALITY

	Evangelical	Charismatic	Sacramental	Activist	Academic	Ascetic
Thomistic (NT)	NT-Evan	NT-Char	**NT-Sac**	NT-Act	**NT-Acad**	NT-Asc
Ignatian (SJ)	**SJ-Evan**	SJ-Char	SJ-Sac	SJ-Act	SJ-Acad	**SJ-Asc**
Augustinian (NF)	NF-Evan	**NF-Char**	NF-Sac	**NF-Act**	NF-Acad	NF-Asc
Franciscan (SP)	**SP-Evan**	SP-Char	SP-Sac	SP-Act	SP-Acad	**SP-Asc**

Legend: **Likely Dominant**; Possible (depending somewhat on introvert/extrovert); Likely Opposite/outline

The point of such a matrix is not to limit, but to free. For example, if a person has been raised with an academic or sacramental spirituality, but has a temperament that is more in tune with a charismatic or an activist spirituality, he or she may feel somewhat inadequate in the work of prayer. Logic, form, and symbol may speak powerfully to others, but this person longs to dance, to draw, or to spend time in a soup kitchen. If we know our temperament and spirituality type, we can be more alert to possible clashes, ways in which to strengthen our current practice, and new avenues to explore.

The matrix can help in this kind of exploration by pointing us to the opposite (shadow) side of our prayer life. If someone is well-placed in his or her prayer life and worship community, comfortable in every respect with "how things are," might the next step of the spiritual journey be to explore a prayer form that is completely opposite and far outside that comfort zone? Like learning to write or draw with our nondominant hand, like learning to "get in touch" with aspects of the opposite sex, learning to pray like an academic might be salutary for the charismatic, just as learning to pray like the evangelical might be for the activist.

Such typologies need to be used with restraint and in good grace. Again, the purpose of all this information is not to bind people with their type, but to set people free to know who they are and to explore more of who God has made them to be.

As for prayers of Adoring, we might begin with the simple affirmation that we are all different, all unique, all special children created for God's delight!

Teaching the Class

The goal of the class is to familiarize participants with the various temperament indicators and forms of spirituality in order to gain greater latitude in their prayer lives.

❖ **Begin the class by playing a song from a praise and worship tape or CD** *(3-5 minutes)*.

If possible, provide a copy of the lyrics for class participants (most praise and worship tapes print the lyrics in the case). Explain to the class that this is the opening prayer, and encourage participants to seek to enter into this time of adoration.

❖ **The main presentation goal for this class session is to overview the material presented in this chapter on both temperament and spirituality** *(20-25 minutes)*.

A handout summarizes this information and should be reviewed as a group, with people encouraged to discuss how they see themselves. If your class took a temperament test, this would also be a good time to review the results.

❖ **It is probably not possible, given time restraints, to explore all of the possible types of prayer discussed in this chapter, and participants should be encouraged to do so on their own** *(20-25 minutes)*.

A prayer form most likely to be left unexplored by busy adults, however, is some artistic expression. Allow an adequate amount of time for this activity, and provide a variety of arts and crafts supplies (for example, posterboard, colored construction paper, crayons, pencils, markers, glue, magazines, scissors, string or yarn, and other art items typically found in most Sunday school closets). Encourage participants to use these materials to express adoration, praise, and thanksgiving to God. You may want to turn the praise and worship music back on!

❖ **Be sure to allow time at the end, or while participants do their art, to discuss how they might express adoration in their daily lives** *(5-10 minutes)*.

❖ At Home This Week

Encourage participants to experiment with various forms of adoration. Some will be excited to realize that their "natural" form of prayer is okay and should be invited to pursue it further. Others will need to be challenged to explore their shadow form. Whatever the case, participants should also be encouraged to continue with their practice of Psalming and Reconciling as they build the movements of prayer into a daily practice of prayer.

TEMPERAMENT TYPES

Thomistic	Ignatian

Logical; enjoys mental challenges; tends to rearrange environment (organizers); leaders; perfectionists; critical; demanding; likely to schedule even play time; communication tends to be precise, with a reluctance to state the obvious, but usually straightforward; future oriented; desire for competency.

Wants to feel useful; typical of givers rather than receivers; practical; work ethic; strong sense of tradition; conscientious; can be pessimistic—"If I don't do it, who will?"; tends to enjoy ceremony and ritual; typical of great law and order people; careful; cautious; accurate; industrious; and always prepared. Michael and Norrisey note that 50 percent of the congregation on an average Sunday will be Ignatians, and so it is worthwhile for clergy (who are less likely to be of this type) to offer prayer forms that speak to this segment of the population.

THOMISTIC PRAYER:

The type of prayer most suitable to this temperament is the logical, rational, discursive meditation whereby the intellect leads one from one proposition to another until a logical conclusion is drawn in the form of some resolution or ethical demand.

IGNATIAN PRAYER:

The purpose of Ignatian prayer is to try to make the Gospels and the scripture scenes become so alive and real to us that we can make a personal application of the teaching or message contained therein. As we enter into biblical stories, Ignatius suggests that we try to use all give senses during our imaginary journey back to the events of salvation history. Ignatian prayer tries to imagine not only what we would see but also what each of the characters involved would say, what the physical objects would feel like, and what smells and tastes might be part of the experience.

EXAMPLE:

Might show adoration by studying it from every possible angle, probably using the seven auxiliary questions: *what, why, how, who where, when, with what helps.* Prayer might then meditate along the lines of: What do we mean by adoration? Why should I adore God? How can I best show my adoration to God? Who are some of the people in the Bible or in history who can give examples of adoration? When and where can I best show God my adoration? What aids can I use to help me in my adoration of God?

Might show adoration by using the "sensible imagination" to journey back into some of the key stories in the Bible, identifying with one or more of the original participants, and giving praise and thanks to God at the conclusion of the journey for the salvation God has wrought. The joy of Miriam at the crossing of the Red Sea (Exod. 15:21), Hannah at the birth of Samuel (1 Sam. 2), and Mary at the conception of Jesus (Luke 1), or the celebration of Joseph on being reunited with his brothers (Gen. 45), King David at the return of the Ark to Israel (2 Sam. 6), or even John in his great vision of the new Jerusalem (Rev. 21)—each of these stories might make a fruitful prayer meditation of adoration for the Ignatian temperament.

Augustinian	Franciscan

CHARACTERISTICS:

Usually creative; optimistic; verbal; persuasive; outspoken; great need for self-expression; tends to communicate with others easily; good listeners; hates conflict; prefers face-to-face encounters; deep feelings; highly committed to helping others; compassionate; enthusiastic; always searching for meaning, authenticity, and self-identity; natural rescuers.

Free; unconfined; impulsive; dislikes being tied down by rules; loves action; easily bored with the status quo; crisis-oriented; typical of good troubleshooters; flexible; open-minded; adaptable; willing to change position; tends to live very much in the present; dislikes practice, and prefers to "just do it."

AUGUSTINIAN PRAYER:

FRANCISCAN PRAYER:

The person who prays this type of prayer is never content with the superficial, external meaning of a scripture passage; there is always a quest to discover "What message is the Lord trying to convey to me in this story?" A spiritual journal, in which thoughts and inspirations are recorded, is a great help in this kind of prayer. Augustinians often feel that they can best pray at the point of a pen.

Since it is easy for Franciscan types to see God in the whole of creation, they are able to make a fruitful meditation on the beauty of a flower, a meadow, a lake, a waterfall, a mountain, the ocean, or any event in nature such as a sunrise, a sunset, or the change of the season. Sometimes a musical instrument, a paintbrush, dancing, or anything that involves movement, action, and the senses can be a prayerful way for Franciscans to show forth love for God.

EXAMPLE:

Might show adoration in a written dialogue of praise and thanksgiving. The last five psalms (146-150) could well be used by substituting the Augustinian's own name or person for any pronoun or personal reference.

Might show adoration with a musical instrument, a craft project, liturgical dance, or any other expression that involves the five senses. A walk through the woods, pausing to give thanks and praise for all that is seen, would be a fitting prayer for the Franciscan temperament.

HISTORICAL TYPES OF SPIRITUALITY

Evangelical Spirituality	Charismatic Spirituality	Sacramental Spirituality

DESCRIPTION:

Centered on an encounter with God through the Word of God. Reading and understanding scripture and seeking and doing the will of God are Christ-centered means of a vital spirituality. Highly interested in personal witness to others with an aim toward conversion. Clear guidelines for living are generally presented and include a strong emphasis on a daily time for reading the Bible and for prayer. Has a strong appeal to the *sensate* type of personality and may also attract more extroverts than introverts.

Focused on the immediate presence of God through the work of the Holy Spirit. This experience is found primarily in worship and praise services, but also in Bible study and small group sharing. Freedom in worship and expression flows from gifts of the Spirit. Raised hands, liturgical movement, a freer musical style, and greater willingness to express emotion are often part of this spirituality. May appeal to an intuitive, feeling type of person, and may attract more extroverts than introverts.

Experience of God known through sacraments, primarily the Lord's Supper, and through the whole of the worship service. Liturgical prayers, usually more formal in nature, and the changing seasons of the liturgical year are part of what helps frame this type of spirituality. Offers structure and shape through the use of a prayer book, a hymnbook, and other traditional worship aids. Might appeal to the sensate, thinking type of personality.

STRENGTHS:

Helps create a passionate, committed, sacrificial, and hardworking person.

Usually leads to a high level of dedication and sacrifice; well able to cross racial and socioeconomic boundaries.

Objectivity—no matter how we feel, no matter the depth or authenticity of our personal faith, the sacraments are real and effective.

WEAKNESSES

A tendency toward legalism and judgmentalism.

Overemphasis on emotion, sometimes to the neglect of intellectual process, and on personal experience, sometimes to the neglect of concern for social transformation.

A dependence upon ritual that can become empty.

EXAMPLE:

Might show adoration through biblical ascriptions of praise and thanksgiving. The focus of such adoration would perhaps be "God's mighty acts" in bringing salvation to people of all times and places. Would be sure to include thanksgiving for all of God's previous answers to prayer and would perhaps even have a prayer list against which to check prior requests and their answers. Such prayer would likely be offered in boldness and in the assurance that God would be pleased to hear it.

Adoration might use the many names of God, likely offered in their original Hebrew, as a way of remembering ways in which God has been at work in one's life. Would probably include singing and/or listening to praise-type music, and might include the lifting of hands in a gesture of *todah*, the Hebrew word for thanksgiving, which is suggestive of action as well as an attitude.

Adoration might draw on the great liturgical tradition of the church, perhaps out of the Book of Common Prayer. Prayer out of a prayer book, far from being wooden and rigid, is offered out of reverence for tradition and as a testimony to the validity of carefully worded prayers that thoughtfully glorify God.

Activist Spirituality	Academic Spirituality	Ascetic Spirituality

DESCRIPTION:

Most often found in the left wing of mainline churches and in religious groups that gather around specific issues (peace, ecology, feminism, etc.). Focus for this type of spirituality is not in worship so much as it is in action. God is met as one serves in society and is politically active. For the activist, the kingdom of God can be glimpsed here and now as we become the hands, feet, and voice of our living Lord. May attract an extroverted, intuitive, feeling type of personality.	Seeking to know and experience God through thinking, reading, and research. For the academic, God is encountered through rational thought, study, analysis and reflection, and that encounter is then expressed in writing and teaching. Probably most attractive to an introverted, intuitive type of personality, and may be strongly represented by, but not necessarily limited to, those who are professional teachers, scholars, theologians, and more academically minded clergy.	Often found in monastic orders and has a Protestant parallel in world-denying holiness movements. Contemplation and self-denial are expressions of devotion to God. A simple life of prayer, rest, and work defines this form of spirituality, as well as a vow to poverty, chastity, and obedience. May appeal to introverted, sensate types of personalities.

STRENGTHS:

High ideals and intention to make a difference in the world.	A search for truth and a willingness to face issues honestly and without sentimentalism or emotionalism.	A strong sense of discipline, humility, and in most cases, Christian community.

WEAKNESSES

A tendency toward losing awareness of God while focusing on activity in the world, thus stripped of spiritual motivation, discouragement is not far behind.	A loss of respect for the holy and a tendency toward cynicism.	A temptation toward escapism and a rigid discipleship that can, in time, become empty.

EXAMPLE:

Adoration would clearly be action. The sense of satisfaction, accomplishment, or peace that follows from a good act done in godly affection would likely be put forth as a sufficient prayer. In this vein the corporate nature of activist spirituality might show itself as the group relives the moment and shares together a sense of thanksgiving and praise.	Adoration might draw on both the activist's sense of accomplishment and the sacramentalist's love of careful words well ordered. The prayer would likely show great forethought and would certainly reflect the fruit of the academic's scholarship. Although the prayer might not be written, it would not be unusual for the academic to pray a prayer of adoration by writing it down, perhaps even as a work of poetry.	Adoration would likely draw on the great traditions of the church. Perhaps more than any other, the ascetic might be best able to see all of life as a prayer, whether liturgical or lived. The rhythm of work and worship observed by ascetic communities is, in fact, designed to make just this point. Thus, the ascetic may make eating a bowl of oatmeal an act of thanksgiving, the simple joy of taking time to notice texture and taste a conscious act of adoration to the Giver of all good gifts.

Chapter Six
Yielding

Our prayer thus far has consisted largely of us talking to God. Reconciling, Adoring, and even Psalming are methods of "answering God" (Peterson). It is time now to be still, to wait, to listen for God's word to us. Yielding is the move in prayer that gives up talking in favor of listening.

The question of how we hear God has confounded Christians for ages. We turn to the Bible and read of lengthy conversations between God and Adam, Noah, Abraham, and Moses. People around us use phrases such as "God told me . . ." or "I heard God say. . . ." Yet few of us have ever heard the audible voice these phrases seem to imply, and we're left feeling like second-class Christians at the mercy of those who "hear" from God.

This chapter addresses the issue of yielding in prayer—or listening—by first suggesting how it is that God might speak to us: through an ideational voice, with ideas that God's creative Spirit sparks in our creative spirit. Next we'll propose several ways that Christians can test what they've heard this ideational voice say. We'll close by making a brief case for being still.

Hearing the Ideational Voice of God

God's Creative Spirit

The Old Testament is full of wordplay. For example, the Hebrew word *ruach* can be translated as "wind" or "spirit" and has a related meaning of "life." It is the *ruach* of God that sweeps over the formless void and chaotic waters of the unformed earth (Gen. 1:1). Later, God breathes the "breath of life" into the newly created being (Gen. 2:7). This rich wordplay is behind the Latin *inspirare*: to be "inspired" is to be filled with God's *ruach*, that windy, life-giving breath of the Spirit.

The psalmist picks up this thread by saying, "When you take away their breath [*ruach*], they die and return to their dust. When

123

you send forth your spirit, they are created; and you renew the face of the ground" (Ps. 104:29-30).

The connection between the Spirit and creativity spills over into the opening chapters of the New Testament. It is the Spirit that overshadows Mary, and once more life is created out of the void (Luke 1:26-38). On the day of Pentecost, God's *ruach* comes like the sound of a rush of wind (Acts 2:2).

The first Christians saw this connection between the Spirit and creativity. Almost all prayers in the early church included phrases such as "Come, Creator Spirit" and "Come, Holy Spirit." It seems that where God is doing creative work, the Spirit is present.

Our Creative Spirit

The Bible tells us that we have been created *imago dei*, "in the image of God." Part of that image seems to be our capacity to be cocreators with God. We create through procreation. We create through art or literature or music. We create when we get an idea for something new, or when we imagine a new reality and speak it into existence. We create when we are inspired.

To be created in the image of God, then, is to carry within ourselves an ability to create. It is this ability—or even longing—to make, to imagine, and to transform that may very well lie at the heart of our likeness to God. Clearly, there are differences! To be God is to be creative in every way and with inexhaustible depth, with the power to create something out of nothing. To be human, on the other hand, is to be creative in a smaller way, with the power to create something out of the materials at hand. In this sense all human creation is really a synthesis, a transformation, of what God has already created. But this ability to create, even if in a limited fashion, appears to be uniquely human. It is this unique ability to transform creation, to bring together diverse elements of the creation around us, that seems to be at the heart of what it means to be made in the image of God (Tillich 1951:256).

Another way to think about the image of God may be to consider that creativity, or imagination, is a kind of spiritual DNA. Could it be that encoded within our deepest spiritual nature, intrinsic to how we are made, there is something that makes us capable of creativity? Could this creative capability, inherited by us from our Creator, be one of the ways (and perhaps the most significant way) that we recognize the image of God when we look into the mirror of the soul? Could this capacity, encoded in our spiritual genes, be the way that we hear and respond to God in ways we have yet to discover, as deep calls to deep?

Deep Calling to Deep—The Creative Process at Work in Prayer

The process of creativity in our lives has been studied by many, but perhaps by no one so well-suited to our concerns as James Loder, who has studied creativity in conjunction with his work as Professor of Christian Education at Princeton Theological Seminary. Building on the pioneering work of Arthur Koestler, Loder identifies five steps in the normal process of human creativity:

1. A conflict or problem that requires resolution.
2. A period of time for scanning—looking over previous solutions and in general processing the problem (either consciously or unconsciously).
3. The inbreaking of an idea that is a new solution, usually made up of elements of previous solutions, but bringing them together in a new way.
4. A release of energy accompanying the release from the conflict, and a freedom to engage in other conflicts.
5. The testing of the idea in the conflict or problem, and a wider sharing of this new solution with others (Loder, 53ff.).

What does the creative process look like in the practice of prayer? One of the best biblical examples is a story about Peter found in the tenth chapter of Acts. Peter is comfortingly like the people we are: people who struggle between moments of faith and moments of doubt, people who know what it is to win and to lose spiritual battles, people who ask Jesus to go away from one so sinful and have tried to walk on water to reach our Lord. Like us, Peter was a common, ordinary, everyday person trying his best to live up to his citizenship in God's kingdom of priests.

We do not have any reason to believe that Peter's prayer life was very much more developed than ours may be. True, he spent several years as a disciple of Jesus, but the biblical record portrays Peter as a man who never quite became a perfect stained-glass saint. If we can read the account in Acts in this vein, it may well reveal encouragement for our own faltering, doubt-filled prayer lives, and help us to see and hear God's word to us more clearly.

Conflict. The action begins with a centurion named Cornelius, who has a vision as he keeps the midafternoon hour of prayer. In his vision he is told to send for Simon the Rock, who is staying with Simon the tanner in Joppa.

We perceive immediately, from the information in Cornelius's vision, that Peter may be in something of a conflict. How is it that Peter, a Jew who has never eaten anything unclean, is staying in the house of someone who, by virtue of his work, is unclean?[1] It may well be that Peter's prayer that next day at noon had something to do with his current crisis: how to balance the hospitality of Simon the tanner with the demands of the Jewish law for cleanliness.

Whether or not Peter's conflict involved inner tension over Jewish purity, what is more to the point is that we seem most often to pray when there is a conflict to be resolved. Conflict, as much as faith, appears to be present in our prayers as the first element of creative process!

Scanning. Peter goes to the roof to pray. Here we see an intentional act of what Loder would call "scanning." Peter may not know he has a conflict, Peter may not understand the need of an interlude for scanning, but somehow Peter understands his need to wrestle with what is eating away at him. That wrestling can be done in no better way than in prayer.

Luke reports that Peter became hungry, and while he waited for his meal, he fell into a trance. A "trance" is the New Testament way of talking about the state of mind of someone who is receiving revelation. There is obviously a close relationship between this state of being "beside oneself," the prayer that creates the conditions for it to occur, and the vision one then receives (so Peter says when describing what happened to him to the Jerusalem leaders: "I was in the city of Joppa *praying*, and in a *trance* I saw a *vision*" [Acts 11:5, emphasis added]).

Inbreaking. The vision involves Peter in a whole new way of thinking about the Gentile problem. It is hard not to use visual language to describe this experience. We would say that Peter has a "whole new way of looking at things" as a result of this vision— that the trance "opened his eyes." In short, he has had an "Aha!" experience.

Release. The fourth step, release, is characterized by a sense of peace, also called ecstasy. It is a connection with God that not only signals the resolution of the crisis, but also frees us to engage in the next conflict. Peter's release is evident as he freely welcomes the unexpected visit of Cornelius's servants (more Gentiles!) and accepts their master's invitation. The curious paradox here is that life in the creative Spirit is not a life of basking in resolution and release, but a life of being free to move from one conflict to the next. To have this be a cause of joy rather than stress is a sign that we have experienced an authentic ecstatic release.

Testing. The fifth step of the creative process, testing (or confirmation), is one that is particularly urgent for us as we take the bold step of listening to the creative Spirit. As we will see, there are a number of tests against which to measure the idea we believe we have received in prayer. Christians can use these tests to discern what is of the creative Spirit from what is of our own sinful spirit.

Peter is blessed to have a double confirmation. First, the Spirit has worked in both Peter and Cornelius. As each risked acting on what he believed he had heard and seen, each was pulled farther and farther into something that offered confirmation and more opportunities for boldness. The synergism of two people interpreting the "ideational" solutions received in prayer back into the original conflict is a not uncommon blessing of the creative Spirit.

A second confirmation comes in the next chapter of Acts as Peter returns to Jerusalem and is confronted by the church there. This is no small thing that Peter has done, and the circumcised community is cut to the heart. Peter tells his story, and when he finishes, the critics are silenced and the church praises God for giving "even to the Gentiles the repentance that leads to life" (Acts 11:18). The drama of the scene is not in Peter's debating skills, but in the holy silence that then bursts forth in praise as the community also sees what God's creative Spirit is doing.

An Idea About Ideas

Throughout the ages people of faith have perceived God in the events of their lives, in dreams, in signs, and in the words of others. But before we can hear God in these things, an *idea* needs to come into our awareness that the ram, the burning bush, the vision or dream, or the comment of a friend is somehow more than it appears—that it is, in fact, the voice or vision of God.

In this sense, while God may sometimes speak to us audibly, God may more often speak to us through our ideas, or "ideationally." This ideational voice of God is heard as the spark of thought that releases the creative tension and answers our prayer. We may call it any number of things—an insight, an intuition, a hunch—but all of these are different names for the same reality: God's vision coming to us ideationally.

In his writing about prayer and discernment, Ben Johnson edges toward this idea about ideas more than once. He tells the story of waiting and struggling in the silence and at last "hearing" a word from God. "This *idea* that came to my mind was not an audible statement. In the silence the *idea* appeared in my consciousness. It spoke to me. It came 'against' me as though it were not of my own production" (1987a:26, emphasis added). He suggests that "God will speak through the ideas that leap into [our] consciousness." After all, he asks, *"Where do you think ideas come from, anyway?"* (1987a:75, emphasis added).

What Are We Listening For?

Each day a flood of ideas comes to our minds. Could some of these be the ideas of God's mind penetrating our own? Could the words that we hear be the tuning of our ears to the voice of God? Could it be that the question is not "How do we hear?" but "What are we listening for?"

Rephrasing the question this way has tremendous impact. How many Christians labor under the misconception that they are spiritually inferior? How many believe that they somehow missed out on enough of God's grace to be "truly connected" with the Lord who promised abundant, as well as eternal, life? Asking "What are we listening for?" also removes the suggestion that somehow our spirituality doesn't measure up because we can't hear God's words to us. Rephrasing the question from how we hear to what we listen for removes the spiritual one-upmanship of people who perhaps carelessly lead us to believe that they actually hear God's audible voice. Maybe they do, and maybe they don't, but that's not really the point anymore. Free from the burden of considering ourselves something less than the kingdom of priests Christ loved us and freed us from sin to be (Rev. 1:5-6), we can forget the struggle of *how to hear* and concentrate more on what *we do hear*. As we come to understand that we are listening for the flood of ideas, that very flood is no longer a distraction but our focus. The issue is no longer: "If I only listen harder, I will hear." Now the issue becomes: "I hear so much! What in all of this is being spoken by the ideational voice of God's creative Spirit?"

Clearly, this is an area for cautious and deliberate reflection. Joan of Arc received rather severe treatment for her insistence that the voice she heard in her creative imagination was nothing less than the voice of God (even if mediated through her saint). Her claim makes sense in view of what we have learned so far, but not every idea that springs from a sometimes selfish imagination is of God. The opportunity for self-deception is nearly overwhelming, and the demand for spiritual maturity is overpowering. We must resist the parental urge to baptize every stray idea to which our heads give birth.

But once we move through these valid fears and concerns, we must also resist the urge to run away from the creative insights that are God's voice because we fear self-deception. Somehow we must chart a middle course that will help us recognize that there *are* times when the Spirit breaks into our consciousness and leaves there an idea that is of God.

Testing What We Are Hearing

Not all ideas are the voice of God. People are routinely arrested with a trunk full of guns and high explosives who claim that God told them to do whatever they were intending to do. As already mentioned, this idea about ideas is a matter for clarity and caution.

Several reliable tests are available to the people of God. Four such tests are offered here as a means of guiding our discernment: *God's Word*, *God's people*, *God's ecstasy*, and *God's boldness*. Let's look at each of these in turn.

God's Word: What Has Already Been Revealed

While it is clear that God's Word does not specifically address every aspect of our lives, it is equally clear that there are some fairly specific guidelines revealed in that Word. The Word of God as revealed in scripture is for us as Christians the rule of faith, a guiding Word that informs our lives.

The guidance of God's Word comes in two ways. First, the Bible provides a fairly clear and extensive moral code. We might call this the reactive principle of what has been revealed: a guide to behavior put together in reaction to situations that inevitably seem to arise in the course of human endeavor. This moral code is drawn from the Ten Commandments, the Sermon on the Mount, much of what Jesus taught elsewhere in parables, and what Paul wrote in the very practical sections of "household instructions" he included in almost every letter.

This reactive principle can cause us to question an idea if it suggests that we do something selfish or to someone's harm or contrary to what has been commanded. Thus, for example, an idea that we kill someone could clearly not be of the Spirit because such an idea is in direct conflict with the moral code that says "You shall not murder" (Exod. 20:13). An idea that we lock a child in a closet to teach him or her a lesson flies in the face of Paul's admonition to fathers, "Do not provoke your children to anger, but bring them up in the discipline and instruction of the Lord" (Eph. 6:4).

The second form of guidance in God's Word might be called the proactive principle of what has been revealed, the rule of love. It seems clear from the sweep of the biblical story that our God is a God of love who seeks our best interests. Although its application is far from clear in every situation, the rule of love can work proactively as we question whether an idea will not only avoid evil, but will also be a cause of some good. Thus, for example, while some might argue that bringing up children in the discipline and instruction of the Lord at times calls for such extreme measures as locking them in the closet, such an argument withers in the light of God's proactive word of love. In this case we go back to prayer and find a better idea, a third option, an idea not born of our frustration and emptiness, but a creative idea born of the Spirit.

The proactive word of love finds its best guide in the life of Jesus Christ. Because we are Christians, all of our ideas—all that we think, do, and say—must be measured by the example of Christ. Understanding this as more than theory helps put zeal back into the words we so easily say by rote, "in Jesus' name." In his book *Life as Worship*, Theodore Jennings Jr. reminds us that true prayer can only be prayer offered in Jesus' name, "compatible with Christ's mission and ministry" and "in keeping with what God has done and promised in and through Jesus" (9). Prayer in the name of Jesus means prayer measured by the loving Word of God revealed in the life of the man in whose name we pray.

In this heady work of hearing the creative Spirit we can never forget that the image of God within us, the image that helps us hear and discern God's will, has been touched by sin. This theological reality constantly urges us toward conformity with Christ as the only means of reunion with what we were intended to be (Johnson 1990:55).

Any idea we receive, as vision or as word, will be verified by God's ultimate Word in Christ. If our idea does not conform to Christ, if our idea cannot be offered "in Jesus' name," if our idea cannot be brought into the light of God's Word, then our idea is *our* idea and not God's.

God's People: The Worshiping Community

God's Word is a primary test for us, but the guidance of the Word is often in the form of broad guidelines. Applying the guidelines and principles of God's Word can sometimes be a Christian's greatest challenge due to our capacity for confusion and self-deception. Thus, God's people can help us further discern what is of God and what, as Johnson calls it, is the "murmuring of our own unconscious." He notes that we are at risk when our spiritual life develops in isolation, "lacking the corrective influence of the community. In the community of faith we share our private visions and personal experiences of the grace of God, and the community listens with discerning ears" (Johnson 1987b:66).

When an idea is tested by God's people, the creative Spirit in the many confirms the work of the Spirit in the one. Beyond the test, however, is the added benefit of coming to a clearer understanding of the idea at hand. Since the many can see and hear the idea with more ideational eyes and ears than the one alone, an insight is often improved as one person's limited vision is enlarged and given clarity by the vision of others.

There is also a confessional quality to sharing the ideas we believe to be of the creative Spirit with the worshiping community. Speaking a vision aloud often helps discernment by breaking the "spell" of the ideas that were purely our own creation and not of God. Could it be that when our Lord says, "What I say to you in the dark, tell in the light; and what you hear whispered, proclaim from the housetops" (Matt. 10:27), it is more than good evangelistic advice? Could this "confession" also be a means of testing what we have heard in the silence of our hearts?

We have already suggested that while our faith is personal, it is not private. Prayer is common prayer or it is not prayer at all, as suggested by the first person plural pronouns of the Lord's Prayer: "*our* Father," "give *us* this day *our* daily bread," "forgive *us* *our* debts, as *we* also forgive *our* debtors," "lead *us* not into temptation, but deliver *us* from evil." At times we pray in an unseen manner, privately and silently, but these prayers, insofar as they are authentic, are also corporate and common prayers. "No matter how hidden, how silent, how private our prayer, it is prayer with the whole people of God—common prayer. The prayer of the community is not the mere aggregation of individual prayers; it is common prayer offered out of our common plight, to our common Lord, for our common hope" (Jennings, 38).

Clearly, God cannot be divided, and God's word to us as individuals cannot be contrary to God's word to us as a community. God's word is ultimately a public—not a private—word, a word such that "all flesh shall see it together." The ideas that come to us in prayer by God's creative Spirit—to us as individuals and as a community—are ideas that ultimately take shape and form as they impact the ministry of the community. That same community, then, must test those ideas.

God's Ecstasy: The Resonance of Spirit and Spirit

Have you ever felt the release of energy that comes with solving a problem? That release of energy is technically known as "mundane ecstasy." It may sound like a contradiction, but the term refers to a form of ecstasy that is a distinctly Christian phenomenon in which we experience more of the ordinary (or mundane) world than we can normally contain. If you've ever had a feeling of being "beyond yourself" or "full to overflowing," then you have had a sense of "mundane ecstasy."

Mundane ecstasy is another way to test the ideas that come to us. In ecstasy we sense a resonance between our spirit and God's Spirit. This ecstatic resonance occurs in prayer when "a union of subject and object has taken place in which the independent existence of each is overcome; new unity is created" (Tillich 1963:119). Such resonance is marked by a rightness of being, a harmony of soul, a peace that passes understanding.

Ecstasy, then, might be another way to talk about the experience of a unique oneness with God. This oneness is an internal sense of having been gripped by the mystery of God's presence in a way that transcends normal human experience. When we hear the ideational voice of the creative Spirit in prayer, when we have been gripped by the divine presence, the knowledge is too wonderful for us! We feel ready to burst with happiness, with well-being, and with love because we have been brushed by the holy. Without some degree of this feeling of ecstasy we have good reason to question whether the voice we heard was God's.

An absence of ecstasy can be further verified by a corresponding absence of fervor and zeal. The resonance between Spirit and spirit releases excitement and energy. The creative Spirit comes as something convictional, giving an energy that drives us to express whatever new idea we have received. In this sense, ecstasy moves beyond a subjective "feeling" and helps us to measure our ideas objectively. Accompanying any energy to express an idea must be a clear understanding of how it can be accomplished. Otherwise the energy will be quickly dissipated, the vision become blurred, and the idea we thought to be of the creative Spirit proved to be simply an idea of our own imagining.

Perhaps measuring the ecstatic energy we feel toward an idea in prayer can best be accomplished by asking whether the idea is profound yet complex, on the one hand, or whether it is simple yet profound, on the other. Ideas that are profound but complex are most easily identified as a kind of wishful thinking in which to gain the fulfillment of the vision we find ourselves saying something like this: "Wouldn't it be nice if this happened, and then this, so that finally my idea could be realized?" The more steps there are, the more wishing there is, as well as the more chance of energy being dissipated along the way, and the more likely that this idea, while not all bad, was probably not all Spirit either.

Ideas that are simple yet profound are more often the stuff of the creative Spirit. Energy can be sustained because it is focused. The vision can be seen clearly from start to finish because there are usually only a few steps along the way. The simplicity of the idea, far from suggesting lack of inspiration, suggests instead economy and clarity. Ecstasy in an idea that is at once simple and profound is the ecstasy of union with a God whose own nature is as simple, yet as profound, as the idea of love. Such profound simplicity is the elegance of incarnational creativity and an objective part of the test of ecstasy.

God's Boldness: The Gift of the Spirit

A final test of the ideas we believe to be from the creative Spirit is whether or not they are accompanied by boldness. Boldness is the gift given by the Spirit in the full certainty that much of what comes to us in prayer will require more of us than we may be willing to give.

The test of boldness is most easily seen throughout the exciting story of the early church in the book of Acts. The concept of preaching boldly occurs in Paul's preaching (Acts 9:27-28; 13:46; 14:3) and in the preaching of Apollos (Acts 18:26). Dramatic accounts of healing, confrontations with powers and principalities, and the courageous proclamation of the gospel in the face of adversity (see especially Stephen's sermon before he was stoned) all suggest that boldness is not so much a common personality trait among the early followers as it is a gift of God's Holy Spirit (Gaventa, 80). In fact, it is a gift that the church in Acts specifically prayed for early in their life together.

> "And now, Lord, look at their threats, and grant to your servants to speak your word with all *boldness*, while you stretch out your hand to heal, and signs and wonders are performed through the name of your holy servant Jesus." When they had prayed, the place in which

they were gathered together was shaken; and they were all filled with the Holy Spirit and spoke the word of God with *boldness*. (Acts 4:29-31, emphasis added)

Madeleine L'Engle, echoing similar sentiments voiced by Teresa of Avila, suggests: "We have to be braver than we think we can be, because God is constantly calling us to be more than we are, to see through plastic sham to living, breathing reality, and to break down our defenses of self-protection in order to be free to receive and give love" (67). God's call to break down our defenses and God's vision for us to be more than we are often come in the ideational voice of prayer. To hear and see this call and vision as God's creative Spirit will demand that we receive not only the ideas, but the Spirit's gift of boldness as well.

The Case for Being Still

What we are aiming for is a time in prayer to be still (Ps. 46:10), to be silent, to yield the floor, to hear what God would speak to us. Such yielding occurs as we understand what we're listening for, the ideational voice of God. But yielding also requires silence.

When we studied the psalms, we talked about the orality of prayer. The psalms were meant to be spoken out loud, not only because they are communal prayers, but also because the spoken word carries a texture, a weight, and a force that is not found in silence.

Another reason for praying out loud—not only the psalms but also our prayers of reconciliation and adoration and entreaty—is to underscore the fact that in silence we are listening. We talk aloud when it is our turn to speak in this conversation called prayer; we fall silent when it is God's turn to speak. The grace is that God may speak at any time. The sin is that we often miss God's word for the sake of our many words.

Getting Quiet

Christians through the ages have used a variety of techniques to encourage waiting. Simply finding a quiet time and place is a big help. Once there, some people find it helpful to concentrate on their breathing. Others recite a simple prayer (for example, the

Jesus Prayer, "Lord Jesus Christ, have mercy on me") or a name of God (see chapter 3) in rhythm with their breathing. Some people have a notepad nearby to jot down things of a less spiritual nature that come to mind ("Don't forget to pick up the dry cleaning today") so they can be released from the mind.

The most helpful method may be to read and reread one of the many scriptures having to do with "waiting for God." This theme is especially prevalent in the psalms, but can be found in both the Old and New Testaments. Here is just a sampling:

Be still before the LORD, and wait patiently for him. (Ps. 37:7*a*)

For God alone my soul waits in silence;
    from him comes my salvation.
For God alone my soul waits in silence,
    for my hope is from him. (Ps. 62:1, 5)

I wait for the LORD, my soul waits,
    and in his word I hope;
my soul waits for the Lord more than those who watch for the
        morning,
    more than those who watch for the morning. (Ps. 130:5-6)

O LORD, my heart is not lifted up,
    my eyes are not raised too high;
I do not occupy myself with things
    too great and too marvelous for me.
But I have calmed and quieted my soul,
    like a weaned child with its mother;
    my soul is like the weaned child that is with me. (Ps. 131:1-2)

But those who wait for the LORD shall renew their strength,
    they shall mount up with wings like eagles,
they shall run and not be weary,
    they shall walk and not faint. (Isa. 40:31)

It is good that one should wait quietly
    for the salvation of the LORD. (Lam. 3:26)

Write the vision;
    make it plain on tablets, so that a runner may read it.
For there is still a vision for the appointed time;
    it speaks of the end, and does not lie.
If it seems to tarry, wait for it;
    it will surely come, it will not delay. (Hab. 2:2-3)

> We know that the whole creation has been groaning in labor pains until now; and not only the creation, but we ourselves, who have the first fruits of the Spirit, groan inwardly while we wait for adoption, the redemption of our bodies. . . . But if we hope for what we do not see, we wait for it with patience. (Rom. 8:22-23, 25)

The injunction to wait, to dwell in silence, is especially difficult for people who are always in a hurry and whose lives are always filled with noise. Part of what we stand to gain in a class such as this is to encourage people to make time for silent waiting. Indeed, as the church looks for ways to be relevant in a postmodern culture, this call to silently wait for the voice of God may be one of the most attractive things we have to offer.

Teaching the Class

The goals of the class are to explore what we are listening for when we yield (God's ideational voice), to learn ways of testing what we hear, and to spend a fairly significant amount of time waiting for God in prayer.

❖ **Distribute the handout entitled "Yielding"** *(3-5 minutes)*.

Open the class by reading one of the texts and then engaging in a period of silent prayer.

❖ **Invite two participants to read the opening skit** *(3 minutes)*.

Actually, only one does any reading. Use your own judgment as to whether you can simply hand this to someone as he or she comes in, or if it would be better to contact someone earlier in the day or week. The skit is intended to be amusing, so encourage the readers to have fun with it.

❖ **Introduce the topic of Yielding by noting that true conversation is dialogue, not monologue** *(2-3 minutes)*.

Yet so much of our prayer is nonstop talking. When does God get a chance? The answer is "when we yield."

❖ **Distribute handout entitled "How Do We Hear God?"** *(25-35 minutes)*.

Lead a discussion following the handout and guided by the outline below.

1) Ask participants to share answers to the question, *"How do we hear God?"*
2) *God's Creative Spirit*
   a) In the beginning it was the Spirit that hovered over the face of the waters.
   b) The same Hebrew word, *ruach*, can mean "spirit," "wind," and "life." Thus, when God "breathes" into the

138

newly created being, it is the Spirit, not the breath, that gives life (Gen. 2:7). In this sense we can say that to be human is to be "inspired" *(inspirare)*, having been breathed into by God.

c) The psalmist picks up this thread in saying, "When you take away their breath [spirit/*ruach*], they die and return to their dust. When you send forth your spirit, they are created; and you renew the face of the ground" (Ps. 104:29-30).

d) The Spirit overshadows Mary, and something unique and wondrous is created: a flesh-word, God incarnate.

3) *Our Creative Spirit*
The five parts to an act of human creativity are:

- a conflict or problem that requires resolution
- a period of time for scanning—looking over previous solutions and in general processing the problem (either consciously or unconsciously)
- the inbreaking of an idea that is a new solution, usually made up of elements of previous solutions, but bringing them together in a new way
- a release of energy accompanying the release from the conflict, and a freedom to engage in other conflicts
- the testing of the idea in the conflict or problem, and a wider sharing of this new solution with others

4) *The Creative Spirit in Prayer*
Lead participants through the identification of these five movements as found in Peter's story in Acts 10 (provide Bibles if necessary).

5) *The Ideational Voice of God*
It is likely that the participants' own answers to the question "How do we hear God?" will provide a link to the suggestion that we hear God's voice in our ideas. Someone will probably have suggested that we hear God's voice "inside our heads" or "in our

hearts" or "in our thoughts." Someone else may say something about God speaking in the events of our lives. In any case, link these suggestions to the master concept that when we get an idea, it may very well be God's "ideational voice." Review the material in this chapter to be sure you understand this concept well enough to communicate it to the class.

6) *Testing Our Ideas*

God's Word: We test our ideas against the commandments, the greatest of which is love.

God's People: We test our ideas in the community of faith, sharing with one another the things we have "heard" or "seen."

God's Ecstasy: This may take a little more work for the class to grasp, but the basic concept is that when we "hear" from God, there is a peaceful euphoria that settles upon us.

God's Boldness: Here again, this may take a little work, but the basic concept is that what God gives us ideas to do may ask more from us than we think we're willing to give. An idea to buy a new sports car is less likely to be from God than the idea to sell your sports car and give the money to the poor!

❖ **Continue the discussion as long as you and the class would like, but reserve time for silent listening prayer** *(10-15 minutes).*

Depending on your group, you may find it helpful to negotiate this at the beginning of class. If it is possible in your setting, move to the sanctuary or some other "quiet place" for this listening prayer.

❖ **At Home This Week**

Distribute copies of the handout "Entreating" (from the next lesson) for participants to read before the next class. There is a lot of material here, and the class discussion will likely flow better if at least some members have taken the time to read through these pages.

Yielding

Be still before the LORD, and wait patiently for him.
   Psalm 37:7a

For God alone my soul waits in silence;
   from him comes my salvation.
For God alone my soul waits in silence,
   for my hope is from him.
   Psalm 62:1, 5

I wait for the LORD, my soul waits,
   and in his word I hope;
my soul waits for the Lord
   more than those who watch for the morning,
   more than those who watch for the morning.
   Psalm 130:5-6

O LORD, my heart is not lifted up,
   my eyes are not raised too high;
I do not occupy myself with things
   too great and too marvelous for me.
But I have calmed and quieted my soul,
   like a weaned child with its mother;
   my soul is like the weaned child that is with me.
   Psalm 131:1-2

But those who wait for the LORD
   shall renew their strength,
   they shall mount up with wings like eagles,
they shall run and not be weary,
   they shall walk and not faint.
   Isaiah 40:31

It is good that one should wait quietly
   for the salvation of the LORD.
   Lamentations 3:26

Write the vision;
make it plain on tablets,
so that a runner may read it.
For there is still a vision for the appointed time;
it speaks of the end, and does not lie.
If it seems to tarry, wait for it;
it will surely come, it will not delay.
Habakkuk 2:2-3

We know that the whole creation has been groaning in labor
pains until now; and not only the creation, but we ourselves,
who have the first fruits of the Spirit, groan inwardly while
we wait for adoption, the redemption of our bodies. But if
we hope for what we do not see, we wait for it with patience.
Romans 8:22-23, 25

Opening Skit

Directions:

Person 1: Does all the talking after the opening response from Person 2, without a break.

Person 2: Follows cued reactions as if trying to get a word in edgewise!

Person 1: Can we talk? I'd really like to dialogue with you about what's been going on lately in our prayer class.

Person 2: Sure!

Person 1: Well, you remember that the first week we talked about the different definitions of prayer, right?

Person 2: *(opens mouth to respond, but doesn't have a chance as Person 1 charges right ahead)*

Person 1: The definition of prayer that I liked the best is the one that talked about prayer being part of our relationship with God. And we all know the importance of dialogue in any healthy relationship, like ours, for instance . . .

Person 2: *(again tries to respond, but is again cut off)*

Person 1: It is *so* important that healthy relationships provide time and opportunity for everyone to say everything that is on his or her mind. How else can a relationship survive, after all?! It's like I was saying just the other day to my friend Pearl. "Pearl," I said, "Pearl, I like our relationship. We can talk about everything!" And do you know what?

Person 2:   *(shakes head)*

Person 1:   Well, I'll tell you what. Pearl just sat there and *nodded* her agreement with me because she knows that we can talk about everything, and we do! That's why I say that for any healthy relationship, communication and dialogue just can't be beat.

Person 2:   *(lifts hand as if to begin speaking)*

Person 1:   Oh, my! Look at the time! Well, it's been *great* talking with you. Let's do it again soon! Ta ta!

Person 2:   *(shrugs)*

How Do We Hear God?

How do we hear God?

God's Creative Spirit
    Genesis 1:1-2
    Genesis 2:7
    Psalm 104:29-30
    Luke 1:30-31, 34-35

Our Creative Spirit
    Five parts of the creative process

       1)

       2)

       3)

       4)

       5)

The Creative Process in Prayer: A Case Study in Acts 10

The Ideational Voice of God

Testing the Ideational Voice

    God's Word

    God's People

    God's Ecstasy

    God's Boldness

Chapter Seven

Entreating

The old-fashioned word *entreat* means "to plead with especially in order to persuade; to ask urgently; to beg" *(Webster's
Ninth New Collegiate Dictionary)*. The New Revised Standard
Version of the Bible translates several Hebrew terms with varia-
tions of the word "entreaty," usually in reference to asking for
"the favor of the Lord."

Many works on prayer distinguish between different kinds of
asking prayer, such as *intercession* (prayer for others) and *petition*
(prayer for ourselves). The old ACTS acronym used the catchall
word *supplication*. Since it starts with an "e" and thus fits into our
PRAYER acronym best at this point, we will use *entreating* as a
fair word for distinguishing any *asking* kind of prayer. When people use the word *pray*, they often mean *entreat*. Many who have
studied prayer believe that entreaty is the primitive beginning of
prayer, the basic, essential heart of all else that happens. Whether
or not we accept this reductionist view, we understand that when
someone says, "I'll *pray* for you," the person means *ask, petition,
intercede, supplicate, entreat*.

This move of prayer raises many questions for the thoughtful
pray-er. Some of these questions might include:

- Is it all right to ask God for things?
- What is the "science" involved in entreaty?
- In what way should we ask?
- What is the role of *faith* in entreaty?
- What is the role of *fidelity* in entreaty?
- What is the role of *fervor* in entreaty?
- What sense do we make of not receiving that for which we've
  asked?

The main teaching device for this class is a kind of catechism
that seeks to give short, concise, meaningful answers to these

questions. The handout entitled "Entreating" was distributed last week. This catechism is reproduced below, one section at a time, with additional material for your reflection in preparation to lead the class discussion.

Question: **Is it all right to ask God for things?**

Answer: **God tells us, commands us, and invites us to ask.**

> "Ask, and it will be given you; search, and you will find; knock, and the door will be opened for you. For everyone who asks receives, and everyone who searches finds, and for everyone who knocks, the door will be opened. Is there anyone among you who, if your child asks for bread, will give a stone? Or if the child asks for a fish, will give a snake? If you then, who are evil, know how to give good gifts to your children, how much more will your Father in heaven give good things to those who ask him!" (Matt. 7:7-11)

Commentary

While it is doubtful that many will come to the class with this first question, it is conceivable that some might be wondering about it secretly. It is my observation that most secret wondering about entreaty and most twisted solutions to the questions about its efficacy stem from the troubling problem of "unanswered" prayer. So it is that someone may have concluded that it is better for us simply to not ask God for things since God appears not to answer in so many instances. For such an individual, a strong biblical statement about God's request/summons/command may be just the ticket.

If we were German theologians, we could perhaps invent a word to represent this series of slashed words in the last sentence. As it is, a German theologian named Karl Barth suggests that while we pray because God has *commanded* it, we do well if we understand this command not so much as divine fiat, but as the act of a gracious God who *invites* us to pray. "In prayer we turn to the God who has graciously drawn near to us" (Migliore 1998:113). For his part, John Calvin entitles one of the sections of his major chapter on prayer "God's command and promise as motive for prayer" (866).

The main challenge for us is to get beyond the idea of "sinners in the hands of an angry God" (Jonathan Edwards) and move to "children in the arms of a loving Father" (Jesus Christ). With our identity as children well-established in the teaching of Christ, we boldly come into the throne room with our petitions.

We will talk more about the problem of "unanswered" prayer later on. For now, let's hold to this image of children with their Father and heed the words of Karl Rahner, another important theologian of the twentieth century. "To lead a truly Christian life is to place one's whole being into the hands of God as confidently as a child takes the guiding hand of its father," said Rahner. "The child's confidence is complete and without the slightest trace of reservation: the hand it grasps is of one who knows best, who loves, who will not lead it into any danger, who will shelter it from evil—but who certainly will not reach down that sharp knife or that poisonous liquid, however much the child, fascinated by the glitter or the color, may clamor to have it. The profoundest secret of the Christian life and of Christian prayer," Rahner suggested, "is to become a child in our relations with God—a child whose quiet confidence and silent submission do not fail in moments of trial when God appears to have turned from us. . . . This apology for prayer will be understood only by one who prays, for it is an understanding that can be reached only in the act itself of praying" (quoted in Kelly, 74).

Question: **What is the "science" involved in entreaty?**
Answer: **A REALLY BIG God.**

It is easy to get bogged down in questions like "If I ask for rain for my garden, and my neighbor asks for sunshine for a picnic, what will happen?" or "If God already knows what is going to happen, and if God loves us and wants the best for us, why do we need to entreat at all?" These kinds of questions, especially when asked against the painful backdrop of unanswered entreaty, can shut down prayers of entreaty altogether. Karl Barth has suggested that God is God precisely because God can work all of this out. While we tend to think of God as really big, God is even bigger, REALLY

BIG. As such, God can make room in the running of the universe for our petitions to actually have an effect on things. God has not only permitted things to run this way, but actually *wills* human participation in the functioning of the universe through entreaty, and all this without giving up any of God's lordship. Genuine entreaty is possible because God is big enough to allow our prayer to be a factor in what happens.

Commentary

The question in this section is really about two kinds of determinism. The first we might call scientific determinism, which suggests that entreaty is useless fantasy in the face of immutable laws (whether God's law or simply "natural law"). The second we might call theological determinism, a kind of superheated Calvinism that essentially concludes there is no need to entreat God because God is going to take care of everything anyway. Although both questions are answered in the response of a REAL-LY BIG God, it might be helpful to look at each issue separately and in a little more depth.

Scientific Determinism. We might also call this the "watchmaker" view of reality. God designed the watch (world) according to certain laws and guidelines, wound it up, and is letting it run its course without further interference. It is deluded to entreat God to intervene and perhaps even rude, an insult to God's great design. This summarizes what we termed the materialist worldview in chapter 1.

We have already suggested that the postmodern worldview is essentially more open to a marriage between science and metaphysics. While many scientists are disinterested in matters of faith, many recognize that the complexity of the universe—its methodical randomness—shows the hand of a higher power.

In his classic work entitled *Prayer*, George Buttrick wrestled with these issues at a time when science was becoming the determinative reality for the twentieth century. He acknowledged that there is some necessary constancy in the world; otherwise, our lives would be "more fantastic than a hall of mirrors." At the same time, the world is flexible even to creatures with as little power as ourselves, such that we are able to alter the course of rivers, remove diseased organs to bring about health, and so on. So then, he concludes, the question is: "Is the universe, so faithful to God and men, and so pliable under man's hand, *open also to the controlling act of God?*" His answer is that God is "constantly busy." In this way, Buttrick defines a miracle not as "something grotesque, not a rending which leaves the natural world in tatters, but an event so shaped by God that it pierces life with His personal meaning" (64-67).

As people of faith, then, we see no conflict between the "unchangeable laws" of science and the God who created that science. "Because there is order and regularity in God's working, it is possible to speak of 'natural laws.' But they are laws of God's appointment, which offer no resistance when he works in new and unusual ways" (Spear, 73).

Theological Determinism. I suggested above that this is a kind of "superheated Calvinism," but for all his bad press, Calvin himself rejected this kind of "predestined prayer" (see quotes in chapter 1 under the heading "Superheated Calvinism").

Karl Barth also rejected any kind of theological determinism. As noted in the catechism, Barth saw God as even bigger than "the hallucination of a divine immutability." The view typically taken is that this immutability rules out the possibility that God can be affected by God's creation. According to Barth, God's immut-ability is as the living and merciful God, not as an immovable idol. God's majesty, omnipotence, and sovereignty consist in the fact that God can give heed to the requests of humanity and find a place for them in God's will. God's sovereignty is so great, suggested Barth, "that it embraces both the possibility, and, as it is exercised, the actuality, that the creature can actively be present and co-operate in [God's] overruling." God's friends have a special kind of freedom, said Barth, such that God will allow Godself to be determined by them, yet without "abandoning the helm" for one moment (quoted in Migliore 1998:118-19).

The response to the big questions of both scientific and theological determinism, then, is that God is REALLY BIG and able to overcome whatever problems we imagine these things create for us. We acknowledge that God has given us an intellect to use for pondering both science and theology, but maintain that whenever such pondering leads in the direction of limiting God, we have pondered astray.

Question: In what way should we ask?

Answer: In the name of Jesus Christ, which is to say:

    ◇ According to the will of the Father
    ◇ In keeping with the Word of Christ
    ◇ In the wisdom of the Holy Spirit

◇ According to the will of the Father

On several occasions Jesus suggested that the will of the Father was paramount in his praying. As we have seen, Jesus taught his disciples to pray "Your will be done," and his own prayer in Gethsemane echoed these words: "Yet not what I want but what you want" (Matt. 26:39; see also John 12:27-28).

It is the will of the Father that the Father's name be glorified. This is not some kind of ego trip for God, but rather a simple, economic statement that whatever glorifies the Father will be the best for the Father's creation. God's loving nature is to will the best for all of creation, and the accomplishment of that will in turn glorifies God's all-loving nature.

It's pretty much a no-brainer that if we could know the will of God and simply give voice to it in our intercession, all our asking prayers would be "answered." The question, of course, is: How can we know all that is God's will?

It may be some comfort to know that many "giants of the faith" share this daily struggle. John Baillie, the great Scottish churchman, once said, "If I thought that God were going to grant me all my prayers simply for the asking, without ever passing them under His own gracious review, without ever bringing to bear upon them His own greater wisdom, I think there would be very few prayers that I should dare to pray" (Trueblood, 109). And Ruth Graham was once heard to say, "If God answered every prayer of mine, I would have married the wrong man seven times" (Dunn, 198)!

◇ In keeping with the Word of Christ

One way we can begin to know God's will is by abiding in God's Word. A rich discourse on prayer found in John's Gospel includes Jesus saying, "If you abide in me, and my words abide in you, ask for whatever you wish, and it will be done for you" (John 15:7). How does the word of Christ abide in us?

The image Jesus is working from in John 15 is that of the vine and the branches, and in this we understand the way it is to be for us. Like that of a branch, our "job" as Christians is to bear fruit. One of the great prayer warriors of the church, Teresa of Avila, suggests that the sure measure of our prayer is not some kind of mystical experience, but the fruit we bear. But like a branch, we cannot bear fruit if cut off from the life-giving substance of the vine.

The bottom line is that we need to be in the Scriptures, and that could be why prayer and Bible reading fit together so closely. It is part of the conversation we have with God: we speak to God in prayer, and God speaks to us as we spend time reading the Bible and abiding in the Word.

◇ In the wisdom of the Holy Spirit

Finally, to pray in the name of Jesus means to pray in the wisdom of the Holy Spirit, deep calling to deep.

Several biblical references link wisdom to the work of the Holy Spirit. The Isaiah text read by Jesus when he first began his public ministry says, "The spirit of the Lord shall rest on him, the spirit of wisdom and understanding, the spirit of counsel and might, the spirit of knowledge and the fear of the Lord" (Isa. 11:2). Paul contrasts worldly wisdom with the "foolish" wisdom of God in Christ crucified, and suggests that he came "not with plausible words of wisdom, but with a demonstration of the Spirit and of power" (1 Cor. 2:4).

Paul also suggests that we "pray in the Spirit at all times in every prayer and supplication" (Eph. 6:18). Many people in traditional churches start to squirm in decidedly uncharismatic ways when anyone starts discussing the person and work of the Holy Spirit. Visions of speaking in tongues and other uncontrolled outbursts make us glad that we are in safe, mainline denominations.

But praying "in the Spirit" does not necessarily mean praying "in tongues." Rather, Paul suggests, the Spirit "helps us in our weakness; for we do not know how to pray as we ought, but that very Spirit intercedes with sighs too deep for words. And God, who searches the heart, knows what is the mind of the Spirit, because the Spirit intercedes for the saints according to the will of God" (Rom. 8:26-27).

So how do we pray "in the wisdom of the Holy Spirit"? Perhaps by asking the Spirit to "inspire" (from the Latin *inspirare*) our prayers. Perhaps by being sure we have "yielded" in prayer before we "entreat" in prayer, trying to hear clearly what God would have us pray. Perhaps by simply being still and letting the Spirit groan on our behalf!

Commentary

This is the only part of this "catechism" that deals directly with the "how-to" of Entreating. This is accomplished by using the phrase "in Jesus' name" as a guide to how we ask God for things. The three "w's" of the *will* of the Father, the *Word* of Christ, and the *wisdom* of the Holy Spirit are all essentially aimed in the same direction, namely, that to ask for anything in the name of Jesus Christ means that this is something for which Christ himself could and would be willing to ask.

The thing to be avoided here is any sense that, if we just say "in Jesus' name" the right way, God will somehow have to answer our prayer. This "magical" sense of Jesus' name is reminiscent of the "hocus pocus" that was inferred by uneducated Christians listening to the Latin Mass (*hoc est corpus meum* = "this is my body"). They knew something special was happening (the bread was "becoming" the body of Christ), and deduced that it came about from the power of the words.

The belief—or more accurately, the fear—that leads people to think that these words must be appended to every entreaty grows once more out of the experience of "unanswered prayer." This ritual is an attempt to get the form right in order to obligate God. It is for this reason that the "catechism" focuses less on the actual words "in Jesus' name" and more on the intent of those words. It is also for this reason that the stories of John Baillie and Ruth Graham are included: there is no guaranteed means for surefire answers (which is to say, the answer that we're looking for) to our asking prayers. Anything that we can do as teachers to pull people away from such superstitious prayer is worth the time and effort.

Question: What is the role of *faith* in entreaty?

Answer: It is important, but the very act of entreating implies faith.

Sometimes people talk about having "enough" faith, as if there were a container inside us that, once sufficiently full, would somehow require God to answer our petitions and intercessions. The Bible defines faith as "the assurance of things hoped for, the conviction of things not seen" (Heb. 11:1), which is to say that faith is the belief God can do something, not necessarily the belief that God will do something. "Having faith" is not so much trying to work up enough belief that God will do what we ask; rather, it is the sure knowledge that God could do what we ask if it is God's will to do so. Since we likely wouldn't be entreating a God we didn't believe could do what we ask, entreaty implies faith.

Commentary

The Lone Ranger story recounted in chapter 1 (see the section entitled "Lone-Rangerism") suggests two opposing difficulties in prayer. On the one hand is our tendency to bypass prayer in order to "do something productive." This is a common problem in the United States, where an ethic of "you don't get something for nothing" drives us to frenetic activity. But some of us have managed to spiritualize things enough to turn prayer itself into a kind of "work." Having "enough" faith, having "enough" fidelity (obedience—see below), or having "enough" fervor (related to persistence—see below) becomes the answer to our felt need to do something.

This line of thinking can also lead to an unfortunate and twisted answer to the "unanswered" prayer problem. And while most of us would deny it and say we know better, who hasn't thought, when a fervent entreaty went unreconciled, that maybe, just maybe, we somehow didn't have "enough" faith? As the catechetical statement suggests, faith is not about an amount so much as it is about a recognition that anything and everything is within God's power. To turn to God in prayer is to have "enough" faith. Once more, anything we can do as teachers to diffuse this secretly held fear will only improve our practice of prayer and our life of faith.

There is an amusing passage from Calvin (who is not generally noted for his humor) that sums up this point perfectly. Giving a fanciful example, Calvin asks, "Now what sort of prayer will this be? 'O Lord, I am in doubt whether thou willest to hear me, but because I am pressed by anxiety, I flee to thee, that, if I am worthy, thou mayest help me.' This is not," Calvin says decisively, "the way of all the saints whose prayers we read in Scripture." He then continues: "If we would pray fruitfully, we ought therefore to grasp with both hands this assurance of obtaining what we ask, which the Lord enjoins with his own voice, and all the saints teach by their example. For only that prayer is acceptable to God which is born, if I may so express it, out of such presumption of faith, and is grounded in unshaken assurance of hope" (864-65).

We, too, should pray out of a "presumption of faith."

Question: What is the role of *fidelity* (obedience) in entreaty?

Answer: It is also important, but beware the "error of earning"!

Like faith, fidelity is important. But we must avoid the errors of believing (1) that if we are just good enough, God will be forced to answer our entreaty, and (2) that if we don't see results, it's because we are bad people. Fidelity is important, and the farther we go in living the life of prayer (a life in deeper and deeper relationship to God), the more important obedience becomes. Yet we are saved not by works, but by grace. No one will ever be "good enough" to force God's answer to a prayer of entreaty.

Jesus said that if we, who are evil, know how to give good gifts to our children, how much more does our Father in heaven desire to give good things to those who ask him (Matt. 7:7-11). Parents love their children and, whether they are good or bad, continue to provide for them a warm home, food, and clothes. But if those children ask for ice cream after a particularly trying time when they have blatantly misbehaved, a parent will probably be disinclined to give them their request! It's not hard to imagine that this is something like how it works with God. Fidelity, like faith, facilitates fellowship with the Father.

Commentary

Like the question of having "enough" faith, the issue of having "enough" fidelity is fraught with danger and difficulty. The issue for the leader is to underscore the importance of obedience while at the same time making a strong pitch for the grace of God.

One of the strongest biblical statements about fidelity is found in 1 John 3:22: "We receive from him whatever we ask, *because* we obey his commandments and do what pleases him" (emphasis added). This verse is often cited in certain circles as a reason that God has not responded to someone's entreaty—that is, the person doing the asking is "living in sin." It is important to note, however, the larger context of 1 John 3:22. Most people recognize 1 John as "the book of love," and the next verses sum up the message completely: "And this is his commandment, that we should believe in the name of his Son Jesus Christ and love one another, just as he has commanded us. All who obey his commandments abide in him, and he abides in them. And by this we know that he abides in us, by the Spirit that he has given us" (1 John 3:23-24).

Belief in Jesus Christ and love of one another are, therefore, the centerpieces of fidelity, not victory over some dark, secret sin. To be sure, a goal of the Christian life is to make progress against these sins. But it is absolutely counter to biblical theology to suggest that God's response to our entreaty is pending our perfection. If it were so, there would be no response to any prayer.

It is interesting to wonder, as a related thought, if fidelity has more to do with what we do after we pray than it does with what we do before. This gets back to the test of boldness we discussed in chapter 6, the willingness to act on what we have heard God say to us as we have yielded. If, in our prayers, God shows us how to love one another better, then an obedient response may set us up to talk to God better the next time around. Understood as response rather than requirement, fidelity does in fact further fellowship with the Father.

Question: What is the role of *fervor* in entreaty?

Answer: It is of more importance than persistence.

No scripture about entreaty is more often misapplied than the story of the friend at midnight (Luke 11:5-8). This story is often cited as reason for persistence in prayer. But a careful reading suggests that Jesus is making a *contrasting* comparison between the friend tucked in bed and our loving, caring Father. This is most clear in the commentary Jesus goes on to give after telling the story: "If you then, who are evil, know how to give good gifts to your children, how much more will the heavenly Father give the Holy Spirit to those who ask him!" (Luke 11:13).

So, how long do we keep praying for the same thing? As long as God continues to lay the burden on our hearts. John Calvin, not often noted for being wildly emotional, indicates that persistence isn't as important as fervor. "Christ does not forbid us to persist in prayers, long, often, or with much feeling, but requires that we should not be confident in our ability to wrest something from God by beating upon his ears with a garrulous flow of talk, as if he could be persuaded as men are. . . . [P]rayer itself," Calvin suggests, "is properly an emotion of the heart within, which is poured out and laid open before God" (891-92). Fervent and honest emotion in a petition said once is more important than vain repetitions trying to fill some bowl in heaven.

Commentary

As is true with the issues of faith and fidelity, people can sometimes make a kind of work out of persistence in prayer. One popular book on intercession even goes so far as to suggest that there are bowls in heaven that must be filled to a certain level before God instructs the angels to mix the prayers in the bowl with fire and then pour them back out on earth to accomplish their purpose (Sheets, 209). The thin biblical foundation for such a view notwithstanding, it once more seems to be a kind of spiritualized Lone-Rangerism: we've got to do something, so we'll just keep trying to fill those heavenly bowls.

As mentioned in the catechism and also in chapter 1 (see "Lamentation Is Always an Option"), the parable of the friend at midnight is often cited in support of the view of persistence. But the parable isn't comparing the sleeping friend and God, it is contrasting them. Ken Bailey suggests that the comparison has to do with the important Middle Eastern concept of honor. The sleeping friend gets up in order to avoid the shame of not helping another; he gets out of bed because of his honor. Thus, says Jesus, if your neighbor knows this much about honor, providing you with whatever you need, how much more honorable is God? When we pray, Jesus suggests, God's honor is on the line if God "stays in bed" (Bailey, 119ff.).

The story of the unjust judge (Luke 18:1-8) is of the same sort. Luke introduces it as something Jesus told about our "need to pray always and not to lose heart." Again, it is clear that God is being *contrasted* to the unjust judge who must be constantly hounded until he grants justice to the widow. It is a message of hope in the Judge to whom we pray, not a message about somehow beating down the door to a God who is stingy with us.

Another oft-cited story for persistence in prayer is Daniel 10. Here we learn that Daniel prayed and fasted for three full weeks before the angel finally came to him. But the angel said, "From the first day that you set your mind to gain understanding and to humble yourself before your God, your words have been heard" (Dan. 10:12). The delay was not because Daniel needed to persist, but because of a spiritual battle being waged in the heavens.

Against all of this misinterpretation regarding *persistence* in prayer, we hold up the idea of *fervor* in prayer. Whether our praying is "free" or taken from a prayer book, the point is that it is from the heart. When God burdens us to entreat, we do so; when the burden is lifted, we stop. What is being suggested here, then, is that our emotions may sometimes play a valid role in directing our prayers. This is not to say that we should pray only when we feel like it (as Eugene Peterson says, "Feelings are the scourge of prayer. To pray by feelings is to be at the mercy of glands and weather and digestion" [87]). Rather, it is to suggest that when we have a passion about something, we should follow it into prayer. Passion more than persistence, fervor more than fatigue!

Question: What sense do we make of not receiving that for which we've asked according to the name of Jesus and with faith, fidelity, and fervor?

Answer: There are several possibilities:

- We can't see what God is doing in response to our asking.
- The answer is either "no" or "not yet."
- Someone else's free will (usually in the form of evil) has intruded.

◇ **We can't see what God is doing in response to our asking.**

There is a wonderful stretch of stories in the eighth chapter of Mark, beginning with Jesus feeding the four thousand (having previously fed five thousand) and concluding with Jesus healing a blind man. Wedged between these two miraculous events, two almost more amazing things happen. First, the Pharisees stroll up and ask Jesus for a sign. Second, the disciples get in the boat and start fretting about food. Jesus has fed almost ten thousand people in the last three months, and here the disciples are in a panic about forgetting a loaf of bread! It's no wonder Jesus had to get away by himself to pray so often!

Jesus' response to all his disciples is that we need to become more "sensible."

> "Do you still not perceive or understand? Are your hearts hardened? Do you have eyes, and fail to see? Do you have ears, and fail to hear? And do you not remember? When I broke the five loaves for the five thousand, how many baskets full of broken pieces did you collect?" They said to him, "Twelve." "And the seven for the four thousand, how many baskets full of broken pieces did you collect?" And they said to him, "Seven." Then he said to them, "Do you not yet understand?" (Mark 8:17-21)

The key to seeing God's hand at work, Jesus seems to be saying, is to remember what God has already done, to notice what has happened before, and to open our spiritual eyes and ears and become sensible.

◇ **The answer is either "no" or "not yet."**

As we discussed under the question of asking according to the Father's will, sometimes we don't see the "big picture," and we must grant God freedom to do something else if God sees fit. Perhaps we could envision God as a cosmic weaver. As we pray, we make suggestions to the pattern that God hears out. Science can see the weaving after the fact and trace the pattern. Great art can observe and glory in the "color and imagination of the design."

But the one who prays stands with the Weaver and whispers suggestions. To these the Weaver replies that some ideas will be incorporated and some cannot, because we do not see the total design in the Weaver's mind (Buttrick, 91).

   ◇ **Someone else's free will (usually in the form of evil) has intruded.**

Many in the church at present are attempting to stand on a two-legged stool. They believe in God and they understand the role of human free will, but they lack a belief in the power and work of an Enemy. No less a theologian than Karl Barth suggested that modern Christians pass over this reality too lightly. "There exists a superior, ineluctable enemy whom we cannot resist unless God comes to our aid. I do not care for demonology. . . . However, it is necessary for us to know that the Devil exists, but then we must hasten to get away from him" (Barth, 73-74).

We understand that people bring evil to bear on their own lives and on the lives of others out of the exercise of God-given free will. Thus, we sense that one who suffers from emphysema and prays for healing while continuing to smoke is exercising his or her free will in a way that binds even the hands of an Almighty God who has chosen to be limited in this way.

What we are less likely to understand is that there is an evil agent, an Enemy, whose only desire is to destroy life. Whether you choose to personify this Enemy as the devil or talk about it in less specific terms such as "the principalities and powers" doesn't matter. What matters is making the choice to see that there is a third leg of the stool we stand on, a third player in our lives who seeks our harm.

It is hard to understand why God set up the world this way, but it is the reality in which we live. We could save ourselves a great deal of pain, guilt, and sorrow if we recognized this to be so and targeted our entreaty accordingly. We can also remember that even Jesus did not have all of his entreaty met in the way he hoped (see Matt. 26:39, Jesus' prayer in Gethsemane), and was able to pray a psalm of lament on the cross (Matt. 27:46=Ps. 22:1). It is comforting to know that God gives us freedom to lament our unanswered entreaty.

Commentary

We come finally to deal head-on with the nagging problem of "unanswered" prayer. As suggested by the catechism, there are at least three possible responses that can be made to this problem.

We can't see what God is doing in response to our asking. Has this ever happened to you? You pray for something or someone—that the cancer will go into remission, for example—and when the person is healed you wonder, "Was it my prayer or the chemotherapy?" In keeping with the definition of miracles offered earlier by Buttrick ("not a rending which leaves the natural world in tatters, but an event so shaped by God that it pierces life with meaning"), it often seems that God's response to our entreaty is not cut-and-dried, but is instead open to both natural and spiritual interpretations. The problem, of course, is that this in turn makes us question the efficacy of prayer.

It is some relief to know that this is not a new problem. As suggested in chapter 1 (see "The Ambiguity Syndrome"), even those who were right on the scene—the disciples and the Pharisees—had some trouble seeing the divine hand in what Jesus was doing. "Surely," we think, "if we were there, we would have seen clearly what was going on." Don't bet on it. Neither the disciples nor the Pharisees were the bumbling fools we often paint them to be. They were intelligent businessmen and scholars, and commonsense, no-nonsense people who knew what side of their bread was buttered. They just couldn't remember where the bread came from!

Jesus tells them, essentially, that seeing God's hand at work in our lives is best done retrospectively. This is why thanksgiving (Adoring) is so important to our prayer lives. In thanksgiving we remember what God has done. As we remember the past we can see more clearly what God may be doing in the present. The theme of "remembering" stretches throughout the Bible, from Exodus to Eucharist.

Practically speaking, this may point to keeping a prayer journal or some kind of list that helps us see how God has responded to our entreaty. We live so fast, so busy, with so many concerns that we aren't sure what God has done because we can't remember what we've asked. Consider challenging the participants to keep a prayer journal for thirty days, recording what they ask God for and how God responds.

The answer is either "no" or "not yet." In many respects we've already covered this in what has been said. The quotes earlier from John Baillie and Ruth Graham form an anecdotal basis for understanding that we don't always pray for the right thing. Sometimes God withholds what we ask for our own good or the good of others. Or it may simply be that the "fullness of time" has not yet arrived. Most folks won't need too much help to understand this particular point.

Someone else's free will (usually in the form of evil) has intruded. We move here into an area that many of us would rather not discuss, and if that is your preference, well then, you're the leader! But note this: a theology that fails to include some notion of an Enemy who seeks our harm, which is to say a personalized evil, fails also to provide people with all that they need to understand what happens in their lives. Follow the lead of Walter Wink (see chapter 1) and call it "the powers that be" if you prefer, but please think twice before neglecting it as some quaint, outmoded, simpleminded notion.

If we are inclined to withdraw from talk of such an Enemy, it is in part because we've seen such talk abused. Whether it is a preacher screaming at a congregation about the horrors of hell or a person who dodges responsibility because "the devil made me do it," we know that the way is open to many wrong turns.

But an even more powerful danger lurks if we withdraw from such talk altogether. As a pastor, I have stood beside too many hospital beds, sat in too many living rooms of families recently visited by death, heard too many parents in anguish over their wayward teen—all of whom have said something like this: "I know God has a reason for everything that happens." The implication, of course, is that God caused the cancer, the car accident, or the drug addiction in order to accomplish some higher good. But really, what kind of God is this? Who would want to worship such a cruel being? No, the answer is that while "all things work together for good for those who love God" (Rom. 8:28), this is not the same as saying, "God causes all things for good."

The risk here is that we are giving up some of our ideas about the sovereignty of God. If God didn't cause this, who did? Well, perhaps the victim. But as former victims ourselves, we reject the notion that cancer, death, or even a drug-addicted child is something of our own doing. To be sure, human free will often plays a part in our own undoing, but not always.

What's left? An ugly scene, if we haven't taken the time to develop a responsible theology of an Enemy. Too many people have left our churches because (1) they can't stomach a God who, by implication, is responsible for all their problems; or (2) they can't bear the guilt, by implication, that they are responsible for all their problems. What's missing is the third leg of the stool.

What if God's sovereignty was not threatened by an Enemy who has the freedom to attack us, but this, like God's willingness to make our prayers a real factor in what happens, is part of God's REALLY BIG nature? It opens up a lot of interesting questions, more than you'll have time to explore in this study, but questions that may lead to healthier and happier practices of prayer and faith.

One of those happier practices of prayer leads us back to the psalms. We noted in chapter 3 that a goodly portion of the psalter is made up of special prayers called laments. The implication seems to be that lamentation is sometimes our only response to the problem of "unanswered" prayer (short of abandoning faith altogether). Moreover, by bringing our lament to God, we have the sense that *God laments too.* God feels our pain, cries when we cry, and is in general even more upset about things than we are, since God loves us more than we love ourselves.

This is a hard idea to wrap your brain around if you're not used to thinking this way. The natural question is, "Then why doesn't God do something about it?" The answer of faith is that God did do something: in a baby, a cross, and an empty tomb. And between the empty tomb and the end of time, granting limited freedom to created beings—whether good or evil—is God's wisdom for our world. I am thankful that God gives us permission to lament about it.

Question:	So, what's the bottom line?
Answer:	**God wants better things for us than we want for ourselves, and entreating prayer is God's idea. Let's get started!**

Teaching the Class

The goals of this class are to lay the outlines for a "theology of entreating"—that is, to understand how we ask God for things in prayer and, more to the point, to understand something about when God appears not to answer.

❖ Distribute "A Prayer of Entreaty" and lead the opening prayer *(3-5 minutes)*.

❖ Briefly revisit the questions from the first week, many of which were likely about concerns having to do with Entreating *(5-10 minutes)*.

❖ Review and discuss the "Entreating" handout, using the areas that are of most concern to the class to guide the discussion (if it was not distributed last week, distribute the "catechistic" piece now) *(40-45 minutes)*.

❖ The experiential time during this session features a five-minute prayer walk through and/or around the building you are meeting in (presumably a church, but if not, adapt the following instructions accordingly) *(5-10 minutes)*.

Encourage class participants to pray prayers of entreaty for members, leaders, church staff, those on the outside who need to come in, and anyone or anything that comes to mind as they walk around (they will presumably know to keep their eyes open for this exercise, but there's always one who doesn't!). These prayers may be said in silence or aloud. Gather the group for a closing prayer after the allotted time.

❖ **At Home This Week**

Suggest that participants do a prayer walk in and around their homes, neighborhoods, and/or workplaces, entreating for those persons and concerns God brings to mind in those contexts. Also ask class members to review the five prayer moves studied thus far in preparation for bringing the class to a conclusion the next time you meet.

A Prayer of Entreaty

Leader: *"Come, let us go to entreat the favor of the Lord, and to seek the* LORD *of hosts."* (Zech. 8:21)

People: **Many peoples and strong nations shall come . . . to entreat the favor of the LORD.** (Zech. 8:22)

Leader: *We pray for all those who are sick.*
We entreat you, O Lord.

People: **Show us thy favor.**

Leader: *We pray for all who lack adequate provision for life: the homeless, the hungry, the destitute.*
We entreat you, O Lord.

People: **Show us thy favor.**

Leader: *We pray for the "hot spots" in our world, places where there is no peace.*
We entreat you, O Lord.

People: **Show us thy favor.**

Leader: *We pray for our friends and family, for the special needs of those we love.*
We entreat you, O Lord.

People: **Show us thy favor.**

Leader: *As Moses entreated the Lord, so do we, saying:*

People: **"O Lord** GOD, **you have only begun to show your servant your greatness and your might; what god in heaven or on earth can perform deeds and mighty acts like yours!"** (Deut. 3:23-24)

Entreating

Question: Is it all right to ask God for things?

Answer: God tells us, commands us, invites us to ask.

"Ask, and it will be given you; search, and you will find; knock, and the door will be opened for you. For everyone who asks receives, and everyone who searches finds, and for everyone who knocks, the door will be opened. Is there anyone among you who, if your child asks for bread, will give a stone? Or if the child asks for a fish, will give a snake? If you then, who are evil, know how to give good gifts to your children, how much more will your Father in heaven give good things to those who ask him!" (Matt. 7:7-11)

Question: What is the "science" involved in entreaty?

Answer: A REALLY BIG God.

It is easy to get bogged down in questions like "If I ask for rain for my garden, and my neighbor asks for sunshine for a picnic, what will happen?" or "If God already knows what is going to happen, and if God loves us and wants the best for us, why do we need to entreat at all?" These kinds of questions, especially when asked against the painful back-drop of unanswered entreaty, can shut down prayers of entreaty altogether. Karl Barth has suggested that God is God precisely because God can work all of this out. While we tend to think of God as really big, God is even bigger, REALLY BIG. As such, God can make room in the running of the universe for our petitions to actually have an effect on things. God has not only permitted things to run this way, but actually *wills* human participation in the functioning of the universe through entreaty, and all this without giving up any of God's lordship. Genuine entreaty is possible because God is big enough to allow our prayer to be a factor in what happens.

Question:	In what way should we ask?
Answer:	In the name of Jesus Christ, which is to say:

> ◇ According to the will of the Father
> ◇ In keeping with the Word of Christ
> ◇ In the wisdom of the Holy Spirit

> ### ◇ According to the will of the Father

On several occasions Jesus suggested that the will of the Father was paramount in his praying. As we have seen, Jesus taught his disciples to pray, "Your will be done," and his own prayer in Gethsemane echoed these words, "Yet not what I want but what you want" (Matt. 26:39; see also John 12:27-28).

It is the will of the Father that the Father's name be glorified. This is not some kind of ego trip for God, but rather a simple, economic statement that whatever glorifies the Father will be the best for the Father's creation. God's loving nature is to will the best for all of creation, and the accomplishment of that will in turn glorifies God's all-loving nature.

It's pretty much a no-brainer that, if we could know the will of God and simply give voice to it in our intercession, all our asking prayers would be "answered." The question, of course, is: How can we know all that is God's will?

It may be some comfort to know that many "giants of the faith" share this daily struggle. John Baillie, the great Scottish churchman, once said, "If I thought that God were going to grant me all my prayers simply for the asking, without ever passing them under His own gracious review, without ever bringing to bear upon them His own greater wisdom, I think there would be very few prayers that I should dare to pray" (Trueblood, 109). And Ruth Graham was once heard to say, "If God answered every prayer of mine, I would have married the wrong man seven times" (Dunn, 198)!

◇ In keeping with the Word of Christ

One way we can begin to know God's will is by abiding in God's Word. A rich discourse on prayer found in John's Gospel includes Jesus saying, "If you abide in me, and my words abide in you, ask for whatever you wish, and it will be done for you" (John 15:7). How does the word of Christ abide in us?

The image Jesus is working from in John 15 is that of the vine and the branches, and in this we understand the way it is to be for us. Like that of a branch, our "job" as Christians is to bear fruit. One of the great prayer warriors of the church, Teresa of Avila, suggests that the sure measure of our prayer is not some kind of mystical experience, but the fruit we bear. But like a branch, we cannot bear fruit if cut off from the life-giving substance of the vine.

The bottom line is that we need to be in the Scriptures, and that could be why prayer and Bible reading fit together so closely. It is part of the conversation we have with God: we speak to God in prayer, and God speaks to us as we spend time reading the Bible and abiding in the Word.

◇ In the wisdom of the Holy Spirit

Finally, to pray in the name of Jesus means to pray in the wisdom of the Holy Spirit, deep calling to deep.

Several biblical references link wisdom to the work of the Holy Spirit. The Isaiah text read by Jesus when he first began his public ministry says, "The spirit of the Lord shall rest on him, the spirit of wisdom and understanding, the spirit of counsel and might, the spirit of knowledge and the fear of the LORD" (Isa. 11:2). Paul contrasts worldly wisdom with the "foolish" wisdom of God in Christ crucified, and suggests that he came "not with plausible words of wisdom, but with a demonstration of the Spirit and of power" (1 Cor. 2:4).

Paul also suggests that we "pray in the Spirit at all times

in every prayer and supplication" (Eph. 6:18). Many people in traditional churches start to squirm in decidedly uncharismatic ways when anyone starts discussing the person and work of the Holy Spirit. Visions of speaking in tongues and other uncontrolled outbursts make us glad that we are in safe, mainline denominations.

But praying "in the Spirit" does not necessarily mean praying "in tongues." Rather, Paul suggests, the Spirit "helps us in our weakness; for we do not know how to pray as we ought, but that very Spirit intercedes with sighs too deep for words. And God, who searches the heart, knows what is the mind of the Spirit, because the Spirit intercedes for the saints according to the will of God" (Rom. 8:26-27).

So how do we pray "in the wisdom of the Holy Spirit"? Perhaps by asking the Spirit to "inspire" (from the Latin *inspirare*) our prayers. Perhaps by being sure we have "yielded" in prayer before we "entreat" in prayer, trying to hear clearly what God would have us pray. Perhaps by simply being still and letting the Spirit groan on our behalf!

Question: What is the role of *faith* in entreaty?

Answer: It is important, but the very act of entreating implies faith.

Sometimes people talk about having "enough" faith, as if there were a container inside us that, once sufficiently full, would somehow require God to answer our petitions and intercessions. The Bible defines faith as "the assurance of things hoped for, the conviction of things not seen" (Heb. 11:1), which is to say that faith is the belief God *can* do something, not necessarily the belief that God *will* do something. "Having faith" is not so much trying to work up enough belief that God will do what we ask; rather, it is the sure knowledge that God could do what we ask if it is God's will to do so. Since we likely wouldn't be entreating a God we didn't believe could do what we ask, entreaty implies faith.

Question: **What is the role of *fidelity* (obedience) in entreaty?**

Answer: **It is also important, but beware the "error of earning"!**

Like faith, fidelity is important. But we must avoid the errors of believing (1) that if we are just good enough, God will be forced to answer our entreaty, and (2) that if we don't see results, it's because we are bad people. Fidelity is important, and the farther we go in living the life of prayer (a life in deeper and deeper relationship to God), the more important obedience becomes. Yet we are saved not by works, but by grace. No one will ever be "good enough" to force God's answer to a prayer of entreaty.

Jesus said that if we, who are evil, know how to give good gifts to our children, how much more does our Father in heaven desire to give good things to those who ask him (Matt. 7:7-11). Parents love their children and, whether they are good or bad, continue to provide for them a warm home, food, and clothes. But if those children ask for ice cream after a particularly trying time when they have blatantly misbehaved, a parent will probably be disinclined to give them their request! It's not hard to imagine that this is something like how it works with God. Fidelity, like faith, facilitates fellowship with the Father.

Question: **What is the role of *fervor* in entreaty?**

Answer: **Of more importance than persistence.**

No scripture about entreaty is more often misapplied than the story of the friend at midnight (Luke 11:5-8). This story is often cited as reason for persistence in prayer. But a careful reading suggests that Jesus is making a *contrasting* comparison between the friend tucked in bed and our loving, caring Father. This is most clear in the commentary Jesus goes on to give after telling the story: "If you then, who are evil, know how to give good gifts to your children, how much more will the heavenly Father give the Holy Spirit to those who ask him!" (Luke 11:13).

So, how long do we keep praying for the same thing? As long as God continues to lay the burden on our hearts. John Calvin, not often noted for being wildly emotional, indicates that persistence isn't as important as fervor. "Christ does not forbid us to persist in prayers, long, often, or with much feeling, but requires that we should not be confident in our ability to wrest something from God by beating upon his ears with a garrulous flow of talk, as if he could be persuaded as men are. . . . [P]rayer itself," Calvin suggests, "is properly an emotion of the heart within, which is poured out and laid open before God" (891-92). Fervent and honest emotion in a petition said once is more important than vain repetitions trying to fill some bowl in heaven.

Question:	**What sense do we make of not receiving that for which we've asked according to the name of Jesus and with faith, fidelity, and fervor?**
Answer:	There are several possibilities:

◇ We can't see what God is doing in response to our asking.
◇ The answer is either "no" or "not yet."

◇ Someone else's free will (usually in the form of evil) has intruded.

◇ We can't see what God is doing in response to our asking.

There is a wonderful stretch of stories in the eighth chapter of Mark, beginning with Jesus feeding the four thousand (having previously fed five thousand) and concluding with Jesus healing a blind man. Wedged between these two miraculous events, two almost more amazing things happen. First, the Pharisees stroll up and ask Jesus for a sign. Second, the disciples get in the boat and start fretting about food. Jesus has fed almost ten thousand people in the last three months, and here the disciples are in a panic about forgetting a loaf of bread! It's no wonder Jesus had to get away by himself to pray so often!

Jesus' response to all his disciples is that we need to become more "sensible."

> "Do you still not perceive or understand? Are your hearts hardened? Do you have eyes, and fail to see? Do you have ears, and fail to hear? And do you not remember? When I broke the five loaves for the five thousand, how many baskets full of broken pieces did you collect?" They said to him, "Twelve." "And the seven for the four thousand, how many baskets full of broken pieces did you collect?" And they said to him, "Seven." Then he said to them, "Do you not yet understand?" (Mark 8:17-21)

The key to seeing God's hand at work, Jesus seems to be saying, is to remember what God has already done, to notice what has happened before, and to open our spiritual eyes and ears and become sensible.

◇ The answer is either "no" or "not yet."

As we discussed under the question of asking according to

the Father's will, sometimes we don't see the "big picture" and we must grant God freedom to do something else if God sees fit. Perhaps we could envision God as a cosmic weaver. As we pray, we make suggestions to the pattern that God hears out. Science can see the weaving after the fact and trace the pattern. Great art can observe and glory in the "color and imagination of the design." But the one who prays stands with the Weaver and whispers suggestions. To these the Weaver replies that some ideas will be incorporated and some cannot, because we do not see the total design in the Weaver's mind (Buttrick, 91).

◇ **Someone else's free will (usually in the form of evil) has intruded.**

Many in the church today are trying to stand on a two-legged stool. They believe in God and they understand the role of human free will, but they lack a belief in the power and work of an Enemy. No less a theologian than Karl Barth suggested that modern Christians pass over this reality too lightly. "There exists a superior, ineluctable enemy whom we cannot resist unless God comes to our aid. I do not care for demonology. . . . However, it is necessary for us to know that the Devil exists, but then we must hasten to get away from him" (Barth, 73-74).

We understand that people bring evil to bear on their own lives and on the lives of others out of the exercise of God-given free will. Thus, we sense that one who suffers from emphysema and prays for healing while continuing to smoke is exercising his or her free will in a way that binds even the hands of an Almighty God who has chosen to be limited in this way.

What we are less likely to understand is that there is an evil agent, an Enemy whose only desire is to destroy life. Whether you choose to personify this Enemy as the devil or talk about it in less specific terms such as "the principalities and powers" doesn't matter. What matters is making the choice to see that there is a third leg of the stool we stand on, a third player in our lives who seeks our harm.

It is hard to understand why God set up the world this way, but it is the reality in which we live. We could save ourselves a great deal of pain, guilt, and sorrow if we recognized this to be so and targeted our entreaty accordingly. We can also remember that even Jesus did not have all of his entreaty met in the way he hoped (see Matt. 26:39, Jesus' prayer in Gethsemane), and was able to pray a psalm of lament on the cross (Matt. 27:46=Ps. 22:1). It is comforting to know that God gives us freedom to lament our unanswered entreaty.

Question: So what's the bottom line?

Answer: **God wants better things for us than we want for ourselves, and entreating prayer is God's idea. Let's get started!**

Chapter Eight
Realizing

The last move of prayer is to realize prayer moment by moment. The idea of Realizing takes up into itself two notions. The first is "praying without ceasing," or as it is sometimes put, "practicing the presence." This notion of realized prayer suggests that we work to reach the point at which our whole existence is permeated by constant communion with God. The second part of this move of prayer has to do with "prayer-shaped action." This notion of realized prayer suggests that prayer will often give rise to some activity, some action, or some announcement of God's presence in the world.

This chapter will look first at the question of praying without ceasing in general terms. We will then turn our attention to how we can discipline ourselves for more constant and consistent prayer in each of the moves of prayer we have studied thus far. Finally, we will briefly consider where we might go from here in the journey of prayer.

Praying Without Ceasing

Is it really possible to pray all the time? Paul gives us challenging words when he says, "Rejoice always, pray without ceasing, give thanks in all circumstances; for this is the will of God in Christ Jesus for you" (1 Thess. 5:16-18). But we sense here an even bigger challenge. It is the challenge of living each and every moment with an awareness of God's presence in it.

As lofty and spiritual as this sounds, it needn't put us off. In fact, there is a basic, down-to-earth sense in which we understand "habitual presence" as nothing more than our realization that we need God *all the time.* Eugene Peterson notes: "Human beings are in trouble most of the time. Those who don't know they are in trouble are in the worst trouble. Prayer is the language of the people who are in trouble and know it, and who believe or hope that

God can get them out." He then goes on to quote Isaac Bashevis Singer, who once said, "I only pray when I am in trouble. But I am in trouble all the time, and so I pray all the time." The "recipe for obeying St. Paul's 'Pray without ceasing,'" suggests Peterson, "is not a strict ascetical regimen but a watchful recognition of the trouble we are in" (36-37).

But it is not just our constant need that makes "practicing the presence" less daunting than it may at first sound. Another and even more compelling fact is the constant presence of God. Consider a scientific analogy for our reality as Christians: we are daily surrounded by radio waves, television waves, and a multitude of forms of radiation of which we are unaware. The only signals we routinely receive are the light rays picked up by our eyes (still a fairly narrow band of the light around us). "For me," says scientist Dennis Sardella, "that's a lot like prayer. I am surrounded by, bathed in, this tremendous reality named God, yet I am largely unaware of him, the only hint often being the wind of the Spirit blowing over . . . the 'heaven-shaped hole in my heart'" (Sardella, 104). Employing another analogy, Sardella suggests that just as seaweed is lifeless, dry, and decaying when taken out of its element, so we too, whose element is to bathe in God, become lifeless, dry, and decaying when we are taken out of (or take ourselves out of) the element that gives us life, God's presence (108).

Discipline That Leads to Grace

There are two inescapable, synergistic, and paradoxical realities about praying without ceasing. The first reality is that we are responsible for developing a discipline for prayer. Think of it as taking responsibility for making sure we are in our element, our ocean. The second reality is that God gives us the grace to undertake this discipline, and even more, God transforms the discipline into a relationship. Think of it as receiving the life-giving power of that ocean without even knowing it. It is sort of like what happens when you try to learn a foreign language. For a long time it is routine: the memorization of vocabulary and verb conjugations. But suddenly, one day, you realize that you're talking to yourself in your new language! So it is in the spiritual life. We work, we are faithful, we stick to it, but somewhere along the line, grace happens.

St. John of the Cross uses the analogy of bird-watching to talk about this mix of discipline and grace. If we don't go out at all or with any consistency, we can't expect to see a bird. Being out, of course, is no guarantee that we will see a bird. But we are much more certain to see one when we have made the effort to be in the place where the birds come.

Our responsibility, then, is discipline. And while this may sound dull and dry and singularly unspiritual, the reality is that grace flows into and out of such efforts. God honors our intention and gives us the grace to keep our discipline. And out of it, God gives added grace to turn that which sounds dull and dry into that which is dynamic and drenched with the Spirit.

There is no substitute for a determined discipline for meeting God. This message emerges again and again in the writing on prayer. Jesus told his disciples to watch and pray (Matt. 26:41). Luther said, "As a shoemaker makes a shoe, and a tailor makes a coat, so ought a Christian to pray. Prayer is the daily business of a Christian" (quoted in Heiler, 119). Richard Foster suggests that even something as mundane as playing a good game of tennis requires that we practice consistently, not just once in a while. "Do we really think we can experience integration of heart and mind and spirit with an erratic prayer life?" he asks. "We develop intimacy by regular association" (120).

Practical Ideas

It may or may not comfort us to know that we are not the first people to struggle with finding the time and tenacity to nurture our relationship with God. The Judaism practiced by Jesus and his disciples included regular hours of prayer throughout the day. When the surrounding culture stopped supporting such pauses in the workday, some people formed their own communities. The monastic creed of *ora et labora* was an effort to provide a rhythm alternating between times of prayer *(ora)* and times of work *(labora)*.

In his classic work *A Serious Call to a Devout and Holy Life*, William Law (1686–1761) proposed using the different hours of prayer for different types (or moves) of prayer as a way for ordinary people to participate in a structured prayer life. His suggestion was as follows:

6:00 A.M.	Start the day with a psalm; offer thanksgiving. (93)
9:00 A.M.	Prayers for humility. (104)
12:00 P.M.	What he called prayers of "Universal Love"— what we would call Entreating. (140)
3:00 P.M.	Prayers for conformity with the will of God— what we would call Yielding. (140)
6:00 P.M.	A time for the examination of conscience at the end of the day—what we would call Reconciling or confession. (147)
9:00 P.M.	Going to bed, suggests Law, is a perfect opportunity to meditate on death! This not only leads us to pray for protection, but also sobers us to the fleeting nature of life and our need for salvation. (150)

Closer to our own time, George Stewart suggested that people pick one activity during the day and associate it with a particular move of prayer. Thus, for example, eating might be the "trigger" for us to pray prayers of thanksgiving; a particular activity of our work, a reminder to pray prayers of intercession; a quiet moment after the children go to bed, a prompting to listen; and so forth (130ff.). Stewart also suggested that several five-minute blocks, spread throughout the day, are perhaps more attainable than a half-hour prayer time (141). Could this work for us? Perhaps we could set aside a five-minute block of time tied to each of three meals, and then set an alarm or some other reminder to stop and pray once in the midmorning and once in the midafternoon or evening. If we were to follow this practice, we would cover our five prayer moves *and* go a long way toward habitual presence.

For many people the demands of work are a ruling force of life. These distractions—or so they appear—take us away from prayer. But what if we could pray our vocation? Richard Foster proposes that this is exactly the tack we should take. He recounts a time in his life when he was asked to dig a ditch, which is not very holy work on the face of it. But with a little effort, Foster was able to turn every shovelful of dirt into a prayer to God (172). Following this lead, what if every memo, every phone call, and every e-mail prompted even a brief prayer—whether of entreaty or adoration—

for the other person? Instead of distracting us from prayer, our vocations could lead us to practice the presence of God!

The demands of parenting are another big part of the lives of many. Finding quiet time in the midst of the many responsibilities and "interruptions" of raising children can be a real challenge. But what if, instead of seeing the demands of our children as interruptions to the quiet, we see them instead as the person of Christ coming to us? Jesus told us that when we receive a little child, we receive him (Matt. 18:5). In place of guilt over not having enough time to "get quiet," perhaps a busy parent could turn each "interruption" into an opportunity to praise God for the gift of wonder in an inquisitive child. My own morning quiet time is often invaded by one or the other of my children. While we snuggle together I take the time to pray blessings over my visitor. Is it overstating the case to suggest that my child's early-morning visit is God's way of bringing to my attention the child's need for an added blessing that day?

There are so many ways to make prayer a part of our lives every day. Whatever our eyes see or ears hear can become the basis of a prayer. We need not be tied to the strict order of our acronym, doggedly working from Psalming through to Realizing. Instead, the events of the day can guide our prayer. The freshness of the new day as we go outside to get the paper inspires us to breathe a prayer of thanksgiving. The headlines urge us to entreaty. The "For Sale" sign in front of our neighbor's house encourages us to bless the family as they begin a new life elsewhere. A lull in our daily calendar prompts us to ask, "Lord, what now? I yield to your will." An unhappy word with a spouse on the phone insists that we call back to apologize and be reconciled. "This," says Foster, "is the stuff of ordinary prayer through ordinary experience" (175).

The goal is one of awareness, of turning the stuff of life into conversation with God. It may be simply asking for simple things or profound groaning on behalf of a hungry and hurting world. It may be simple praise for simple pleasures or wordless wonder at God's majesty. It may be a quiet moment in the car or an hour blocked out of our weekly schedule to head to the church sanctuary and there wait for God with a listening heart. It may not be the most natural thing for us to do at first, but by God's grace and our own determined discipline, we work to talk to God, instead of just to our lonely selves, about everything that is happening to us and around us.

Practicing the Presence in PRAYER

Having discussed praying without ceasing in general terms, we turn our attention now to thinking about the specific moves of prayer we have been studying. The question before the class will be to review the substance of each movement and then suggest two or three ways of realizing God's presence in that movement throughout the day.

Psalming

While we might look at the psalms only as part of a set-apart time with God (and thus, when we might be likely to have a Bible handy), their force can stay with us throughout the day, providing a place to put some of our anger and frustration. Walter Brueggemann suggests that we tend to use the psalms only in our "equilibrium"—that is, we pray them only as prayers of praise and well-being. In so doing we miss the point and power of the psalms, which are really better understood as speeches of "disequilibrium," as prayers of pain and sorrow. Many of the psalms reflect where most of us live our lives; they are in touch with the raw edges, the deep hurts, and the unrestrained passions that always lurk nearby. "For most of us," says Brueggemann, "liturgical or devotional entry into the Psalms requires a real change of pace. It asks us to depart from the closely managed world of public survival, to move into the open, frightening, healing world of speech with the Holy One" (1982:20).

This being the case, we do well to know the psalms and keep them close. Throughout the day we may find more than one occasion to ask, "How long, O Lord?"

Reconciling

The prompting for immediate prayer can and should always be the quick recognition of the need for confession in our lives. As suggested above, the "trigger" is seeing that something has gone amiss and needs to be reconciled or made right. "Specific confession of sins cannot . . . wait for an appointed time," suggests Stewart. "It follows swiftly on the knowledge of transgression, the more swiftly the better. Any act of redress which you can make is more readily offered, and more surely accepted before there is time to brood over it, and absorption in the day's work to reduce a keen regret to a dull uneasiness. Never delay the cry to God for pardon and cleansing" (30-31).

In this regard we should also note the value of prayer as a preventative to temptation. Elton Trueblood has observed that when temptation comes, it is usually already too late: "The decision whether or not to yield to temptation has already been deeply influenced by prior decisions, and by prior preparations for moral defense. Unless we arm ourselves in advance of the moral battle, we have very little chance when finally the actual test occurs." Trueblood goes on to quote John Baillie, who said, "Prayer is *the soul's vigil.*" Says Trueblood, "Our best chance of escape from moral danger lies in the act of prayerful preparedness." "So it is that sin is conquered," Baillie said, "not in the moment of temptation but in the long prayerful discipline that precedes it" (60-61).

Adoring

Paul's admonition to "pray without ceasing" is couched in the larger language of the primacy of praise: "Rejoice always, pray without ceasing, give thanks in all circumstances; for this is the will of God in Christ Jesus for you" (1 Thess. 5:16-18). Paul seems to be saying that an attitude of adoration should be the primary stance of Christians in the world.

For all of their language of lament, the psalms support the primacy of praise.

> Make a joyful noise to the LORD, all the earth.
>   Worship the LORD with gladness;
>   come into his presence with singing.
> Know that the LORD is God.
>   It is he that made us, and we are his;
>   we are his people, and the sheep of his pasture.
> Enter his gates with thanksgiving, and his courts with praise.
>   Give thanks to him, bless his name. (Ps. 100:1-4)

The way to come into God's presence is through joyful noise, worship, singing, thanksgiving, and praise—in short, through Adoring our God, regardless of how we feel. But a double meaning is at work here: not only is praise the fitting way to *come into* God's presence, but the psalm also allows for the idea that as we praise, we are *drawn into* God's presence. This may be one of the most important but overlooked truths of corporate worship: not only do we praise God as a response, but we also praise God as a point of entry. Praise, we could say, is the key to the gate of God's courts.

Adopting an attitude of praise throughout the day is ostensibly made more or less difficult by our situations. Yet often the most thankful people are those who would appear to others to be the most beset. The person who is "content" is probably the one who needs an intentional infusion of Adoring. This can be had simply by opening eyes, ears, and hearts to the awesome reality of God all around us. The singing of birds or the patter of rain, the freshness of a new day and of life itself, the warmth of the sheets, and the promise of what lies ahead—all of these are cause for Adoring even before getting out of bed!

Yielding

Of all the moves of prayer we have discussed, none is more important for us than the prayer of Yielding. It is here that we become quiet and listen for God.

This being said, Yielding prayer is probably also the hardest to achieve throughout the day. Even if we manage to get away from the noise and distraction going on around us, we encounter the noise and distraction going on inside us. Yet this is not a reason to lose heart. George Stewart suggests that distraction in our praying is not altogether bad, that in fact there is much to be learned from it. Thus, for example, "the joyous excitement which unsettled us becomes a part of thanksgiving. The sorrow or fear which disturbed us adds earnestness to our petitions. The injury or annoyance enters into our prayers as intercession for him who did us wrong, or becomes a part of our penitence for our own evil." Stewart concludes: "When we can make our distractions become vital parts of our prayers, they are no longer hindrances but spiritual influences of good" (50).

Of course, in the midst of what we find distracting, we might also find a word from God. We spoke about God's ideational voice, and learning to hear this voice amidst the many others around us is part of our Christian joy. Although we may not be able to "get quiet" during the day, we can recognize that an idea has come to us and then use that as the "trigger" to engage the Lord in prayerful conversation. Saying something like "Lord, I've just had an idea, is this from you?" followed by a pause to listen further may lead to a response far more abundant than all we can ask or imagine (Eph. 3:20).

Entreating

Most of us won't have any problem making entreaty a regular part of our prayer lives, and that's okay! Richard Foster suggests that anyone who demeans the asking dimension of prayer as somehow "less spiritual" has succumbed to a lesser spirituality. The Lord's Prayer is all entreaty, even down to asking God only for "daily bread." The implication is that we'll be back the next day to ask again, and the further implication is that that's the way God likes it!

We've already suggested that what we see and hear feeds our adoration of God. The same is true for our Entreating. When we read the newspaper or hear a siren, we can "pray the day" by being attentive to what happens to and around us (Egan, 16). It is not hard to imagine that, being mindful (which is to say, prayerful) about all that goes on around each of us every day, we should easily be able to pray without ceasing, with our prayer being a constant stream of either adoration or entreaty.

Realizing

We've been talking thus far about Realizing in its first sense, as "praying without ceasing" or "practicing the presence." But a second way to understand Realizing is as "prayer-shaped action." This notion of realized prayer suggests that prayer will often give rise to some activity, some action, or some announcement of God's presence in the world.

The reality is that when we pray, we will be moved to act as well. Part of discerning is learning what things God would have us act on and what things belong to someone else's activity. But it is likely that while we entreat for the famine victims, we will feel the urge to send some kind of famine relief. It is likely that as we are about the business of Reconciling, we'll get some clear idea of how to accomplish the human part of what is needed. And how often has someone's Adoring given rise to a poem, a song, or a sketch or drawing? Prayer leads to action; action calls us back to prayer.

There is clearly a tension here. On the one hand, we want to avoid the attitude that looks with disdain on any kind of activity that is not overtly holy. On the other hand, we want to avoid the attitude that says, "I don't have time to pray; I have to *do* something." The real road, the right road, is somewhere in between. "Total involvement in prayer demands of us a participation in society, in the lives of those close to us, of those at a distance, of intimate friends, and of strangers" (Ellul, 170).

As we fold our hands in prayer we should note our dirty fingernails. Prayer should never be used as an excuse for not serving in the soup kitchen, teaching a literacy class, or building a Habitat for Humanity house. Nor should any of these activities be undertaken without thorough covering in prayer; they should not be mentioned merely as a toss-off at the start to satisfy the "prayer requirement." Prayer calls to action; action calls us back to prayer.

In this regard we should also mention the prayer of the Little Way developed by Thérèse of Lisieux. Her insight was "to seek out the menial job, to welcome unjust criticisms, to befriend those who annoy us, to help those who are ungrateful." Thérèse believed that these "trifles" were more pleasing to Jesus than great and holy deeds. "The beauty of the Little Way is how utterly available it is to everyone. . . . The opportunities to live in this way come to us constantly, while the great fidelities happen only now and again. Almost daily we can give smiling service to nagging co-workers, listen attentively to silly bores, express little kindnesses without making a fuss" (Foster, 62).

Where Do We Go from Here?

There is an old book on prayer by George Stewart that I have quoted several times. The book's title would never sell today. It's called *The Lower Levels of Prayer*. What is fascinating about the title, however, is what it implies—namely, that there are different *levels* of prayer, some lower, some higher.

While we may be reluctant to admit this (it sounds so politically incorrect, after all), it speaks of a truth we recognize. In fact, what scares many people away from prayer is the notion that somehow they have to be expert in it to do it at all. The truth, as we've come to see, is that anyone can pray, that there are various kinds of prayers, and that God is eager to hear them all. An analogy might be the parent who works so hard to hear the child's first words and makes a great fuss over those words, even though the words are likely to be only "Mama" or "Dada." Can we doubt that God is equally thrilled to hear our simple words?

The analogy breaks down, however, if we equate physical growth with spiritual growth. If a "grown-up" believes that he or she should be "grown-up" in prayer as well, and then either imposes an immature understanding of prayer on others or hides the fact of that immaturity behind a false spirituality, the church suffers. There is no shame in admitting we aren't grown-up yet; the greater shame is in not realizing we may still need to grow. "An apprentice electrician is not allowed to do the tasks of a journeyman," suggests Foster, "because he is not ready for those tasks, and for him to undertake them could, in fact, be dangerous. So it is in the spiritual life. We must learn our multiplication tables before we attempt calculus, so to speak. This is simply a fact of the spiritual realm" (156).

All of this is to say that there is no shame in not yet being grown-up in prayer, in learning first about the "lower levels" of prayer, *so long as we aren't content to stay there!* As far as we know, there is no end to the spiritual journey this side of heaven; we can always be doing something to deepen our relationship with God through Jesus Christ in the power of the Holy Spirit.

Good Reading

So where do we go from here? First, keep reading. There are many good books listed in the bibliography. Among those most highly recommended would be the following:

*P*salming

Roberta C. Bondi's *A Place to Pray: Conversations on the Lord's Prayer*
Eugene Peterson's *Answering God: The Psalms as Tools for Prayer*

*R*econciling

L. Gregory Jones's *Embodying Forgiveness*

*A*doring

Malcolm Goldsmith's *Knowing Me, Knowing God*

*Y*ielding

Richard Foster's *Prayer*

*E*ntreating

Terry Teykl's *Pray the Price*

*R*ealizing

Walter Wink's *The Powers That Be*

In terms of general reading on prayer, Ben Johnson's *To Pray God's Will, To Will God's Will,* and *Discerning God's Will* make an important trilogy, and Avery Brooke's eminently readable book *Healing in the Landscape of Prayer* is a good primer for those interested in reading more about healing.

The Community in Prayer

The second thing we might do in answering where we go from here is to look again at the communal life of prayer. Many Christians place a high priority on "getting away with God." Withdrawing into the prayer closet, going up on the prayer mountain, having a private quiet time—all of these are held up as the pinnacle of the spiritual life.

Yet this may be only half of the story.

I argued in the introduction that there is much confusion between the words "private" and "personal" in the spiritual life. While one's life with God has a deeply personal aspect, the biblical witness, taken as a whole, argues against a private spirituality. Yes, Jesus withdrew to the mountain to pray, but he always returned to his disciples and the larger crowds. Even when Jesus went to Gethsemane to be in deep and desperate conversation with his Father, the disciples were not far away.

We see this most clearly in the use of the first person plural in the Lord's Prayer. "*Our* Father . . . give us this day *our* daily bread . . . forgive *us our* sins . . . lead *us* not into temptation." The Lord's Prayer is not a prayer that can be well-prayed alone. As a model for all our praying, it suggests that prayer is fundamentally a corporate activity.

Perhaps our need for the solitude of a private prayer time grows out of a dissatisfaction with how corporate prayer is usually done. This may suggest that, instead of retreat and escape, we should reexamine how we pray together. For example, what if prayer started with a time of enthusiastic adoration, our praise and thanksgiving ushering us into the throne room of God? What if, in preparation for this, each person came to the meeting prepared to share something, as Paul suggests in 1 Corinthians 14:26: "When you come together, each one has a hymn, a lesson, a revelation, a tongue, or an interpretation. Let all things be done for building up"? I once led a prayer meeting like this, and it was amazing to see what people brought: one woman played "Amazing Grace" on a small psaltery, another brought a reading from a great spiritual classic. One man brought a "tongue" as he read from his German Bible and then provided the interpretation, while another man wrote a song and played guitar. All of this from people away on a retreat with only a simple invitation the day before. Imagine what would be possible if week by week people came to the "prayer meeting" with this kind of creative excitement in adoring God together!

And what if, rather than going around the room sharing prayer concerns for twenty minutes and then praying about them for five, we instead went right to prayer? What if the people who had these concerns shared them in prayer, their emotion fueling their cries for help? Then, in response, the group had a covenant that at least one or two others would "jump on" that cry for help and pray with and for their brother or sister?

And what if, having exhausted ourselves in adoration and

entreaty, we waited together in silence? There are few things as powerful as sustained corporate silence in prayer, where each person has moved past the awkwardness of growling stomachs and squeaky air conditioners, where people know that while they are meeting personally with God, they are not meeting privately but corporately. As the presence of God settles over such a gathering, amazing things begin to take place.

The early church knew the central importance of the gathering, of constituting the Body of Christ. It is sobering to note that Jesus didn't say, "Where one is gathered, there I am in the midst of them." To be sure, Jesus is present with us everywhere, but our God is radically relational, even down to being a Trinity within Godself. Perhaps it is time the church rediscovered this radical relationality as we seek more and more to realize prayer.

Teaching the Class

The goals of the class are to overview the six moves of prayer, to brainstorm together ways of Realizing prayer in each moment of our lives, and through this discussion to gain insight into the spiritual life.

❖ **Distribute the handout entitled "The Practice of Prayer"** *(3-5 minutes).*

For the opening prayer, ask students to lead brief prayers based on one of these scriptural affirmations about prayer.

❖ **Distribute the worksheet entitled "Putting It All Together"** *(25-30 minutes).*

Review each movement of prayer and brainstorm ways of Realizing each movement throughout a normal day or week.

❖ **Lead a time of sharing and discussion on what it means to live "a life attuned to God"** *(10-15 minutes).*

This is essentially a time to reflect on making prayer more and more a part of our lives, and looking ahead to where we can go from here.

❖ **Distribute the "Evaluation" worksheet and allow participants time to complete it** *(5 minutes).*

❖ **Select a prayer option to close the prayer time.**

The leader could simply lead a prayer (the least desirable option!), or participants could volunteer to offer one type of prayer (i.e., Psalming, Reconciling, Adoring, Yielding [silence], Entreating). Do what seems right for the group on this last occasion together.

The Practice of Prayer

The following are biblical affirmations about prayer. Please choose one and reflect on it silently. During our prayer time in a few minutes, as you feel led, please consider offering a brief prayer based on what your chosen verse says.

We believe:

♦ that we should rejoice in hope, be patient in suffering, and persevere in prayer. (Rom. 12:12)

♦ that the Spirit helps us in our weakness; for we do not know how to pray as we ought, but that very Spirit intercedes with sighs too deep for words. (Rom. 8:26)

♦ that if any among us is suffering, they should pray, if any are cheerful, they should sing songs of praise, and if any among us is sick, they should call for the elders of the church and have them pray over them, anointing them with oil in the name of the Lord. (James 5:13-14)

♦ that we should rejoice always, pray without ceasing, give thanks in all circumstances; for this is the will of God in Christ Jesus for us. (1 Thess. 5:16-18)

♦ that we should pray in the Spirit at all times in every prayer and supplication. (Eph. 6:18a)

♦ that we should not worry about anything, but in everything by prayer and supplication with thanksgiving let our requests be made known to God. (Phil. 4:6)

♦ that we should devote ourselves to prayer, keeping alert in it with thanksgiving. (Col. 4:2)

♦ that in every place people should pray, lifting up holy hands without anger or argument. (1 Tim. 2:8)

♦ that the end of all things is near; therefore we should be serious and discipline ourselves for the sake of our prayers. (1 Pet. 4:7)

♦ that we should build ourselves up on our most holy faith and pray in the Holy Spirit. (Jude 20)

Putting It All Together

We have studied five movements in prayer: *Psalming, Reconciling, Adoring, Yielding,* and *Entreating.* Review the substance of each movement and then suggest two or three ways of *Realizing* God's presence in that movement throughout the day.

*P*salming

*R*econciling

*A*doring

*Y*ielding

*E*ntreating

*R*ealizing

Evaluation

What are the most important or meaningful things you've learned as a result of this class?

Is there something you are still wondering about in regard to prayer that wasn't covered or remains unclear after taking this class?

What would you do to improve this class?

What one thing would you suggest be left unchanged if it were taught again?

Other comments/concerns:

Thanks!

Notes

Introduction

1. *Please Understand Me* is available from Prometheus Nemesis Book Company, Box 2748, Del Mar, CA 29014; (706) 632-1575. The test can be purchased separately at nominal cost from the same address. Please note that delivery time is estimated at four weeks.

Chapter 1. Prayer in the Postmodern Era

1. The Freudian legacy for postmodern people is not so much the idea that there is no God and so in prayer I talk only to myself. Rather, Freud's critique is that prayer represents *"an evasion of my self* . . . an alienation from my own motives and desires by projecting them outward. Not that there is no God, but that the God of my address is my own creation, and that out of my own most childish fears and needs. . . . What is novel is the analysis of this constructive activity as neurotic, an enterprise of arrested development. The moral critique of prayer, at least as old as Rousseau's Vicar of Savoy, is driven home in a new way by Freud's hermeneutics of suspicion" (McDargh, 78).
2. "Prayer" in what follows should be understood mostly as "entreaty." It is the "asking for things" part of prayer that raises most of these questions.
3. Taken from *The Book of Confessions*. Louisville, Ky.: Office of the General Assembly, Presbyterian Church (U.S.A.), 1999.

Chapter 2. The Lord's Prayer as Pattern

1. The best solution is probably "glorify your name" as in John 12:28, but that still doesn't provide quite the shock we need in terms of the instrumentality of our prayers.
2. John Baillie said, "If I thought that God were going to grant

me all my prayers simply for the asking, without ever passing them under His own gracious review, without ever bringing to bear upon them His own greater wisdom, I think there would be very few prayers that I should dare to pray" (quoted in Trueblood, 109).

3. See Lea, *Could You Not Tarry One Hour?*, pp. 55-164; Purdy, *Lord, Teach Us to Pray*, pp. 2-3; and Arthur, *Lord, Teach Me to Pray in 28 Days*, p. 26.

4. Taken from *The Presbyterian Hymnal*. Louisville, Ky.: Westminster John Knox Press, 1990, p. 16. English translation of the Lord's Prayer prepared by the English Language Liturgical Consultation (ELLC), 1988.

Chapter 3. Psalming

1. These "problems" with the psalms are only such for us as modern readers. In their original setting the psalms made perfect sense and were likely ordered in a way that everyone understood.

Chapter 4. Reconciling

1. See chapter 1.

Chapter 6. Yielding

1. A tanner handled dead animals and would therefore be ritually impure almost all of the time.

Bibliography

Allen, Diogenes
1997   *Spiritual Theology.* Boston, Mass.: Cowley
               Publications.

Arthur, Kay
1982   *Lord, Teach Me to Pray in 28 Days.* Eugene,
               Ore.: Harvest House Publishers.

Bailey, Kenneth E.
1976   *Poet & Peasant; and, Through Peasant Eyes.*
               Grand Rapids, Mich.: William B. Eerdmans
               Publishing Company.

Barth, Karl
1952   *Prayer.* Philadelphia, Pa.: The Westminster Press.

Bondi, Roberta C.
1998   *A Place to Pray: Reflections on the Lord's Prayer.*
               Nashville, Tenn.: Abingdon Press.

Brooke, Avery
1996   *Healing in the Landscape of Prayer.* Boston,
               Mass.: Cowley Publications.

Brueggemann, Walter
1982   *Praying the Psalms.* Winona, Minn.: Saint Mary's
               Press.
1984   *The Message of the Psalms: A Theological
               Commentary.* Minneapolis, Minn.: Augsburg
               Publishing House.
1993   *Texts Under Negotiation: The Bible and
               Postmodern Imagination.* Minneapolis, Minn.:
               Fortress Press.

Buttrick, George A.
1942   *Prayer*. New York, N.Y.: Abingdon Press.

Calvin, John
1960   *The Library of Christian Classics Vol. XXI—Calvin: Institutes of the Christian Religion*. Ed. John T. McNeill. Philadelphia, Pa.: The Westminster Press.

Carson, D. A., ed.
1990   *Teach Us to Pray*. London: World Evangelical Fellowship.

Charlesworth, James H.
1993   "Jewish Prayers in the Time of Jesus" in Daniel L. Migliore, ed. *The Lord's Prayer: Perspectives for Reclaiming Christian Prayer*. Grand Rapids, Mich.: William B. Eerdmans Publishing Company.

Church, F. Forrester and Terrence T. Mulry, eds.
1988   *The Macmillan Book of Earliest Christian Prayers*. New York, N.Y.: Collier Macmillan.

Donnelly, Doris
1979   *Learning to Forgive*. New York, N.Y.: Macmillan Publishing Co., Inc.

Dunn, Ronald
1992   *Don't Just Stand There, Pray Something*. Nashville, Tenn.: Thomas Nelson Publishers.

Ebeling, Gerhard
1966   *On Prayer: The Lord's Prayer in Today's World*. Philadelphia, Pa.: Fortress Press.

Egan, Harvey D., S.J.
1991   "A Jesuit Looks at Jesuit Prayer" in William A. Barry and Kerry A. Maloney, eds. *A Hunger for*

God: Ten Approaches to Prayer. Kansas City, Mo.: Sheed & Ward.

Ellul, Jacques
1970   *Prayer and Modern Man.* New York, N.Y.: The Seabury Press.

Foster, Richard J.
1992   *Prayer: Finding the Heart's True Home.* San Francisco, Calif.: HarperCollins Publishers.

Froehlich, Karlfried
1993   "The Lord's Prayer in Patristic Literature" in Daniel L. Migliore, ed. *The Lord's Prayer: Perspectives for Reclaiming Christian Prayer.* Grand Rapids, Mich.: William B. Eerdmans Publishing Company.

Gaventa, Beverly
1986   "To Speak Thy Word with All Boldness, Acts 4:23-31." *Faith and Mission* 3:76-82.

Goldsmith, Malcolm
1997   *Knowing Me, Knowing God: Exploring Your Spirituality with Myers-Briggs.* Nashville, Tenn.: Abingdon Press.

Heiler, Friedrich
1958   *Prayer: A Study in the History and Psychology of Religion.* New York: Oxford University Press.

Hooper, Patricia
1997   "Prayer." *Atlantic Monthly* (June).

Hubbard, David Allan
1983   *The Practice of Prayer: A Guide for Beginners.* Downers Grove, Ill.: InterVarsity Press.

Jennings, Jr., Theodore W.
1982   *Life as Worship: Prayer and Praise in Jesus' Name.* Grand Rapids, Mich.: William B. Eerdmans Publishing Company.

Johnson, Ben C.
1987a   *To Pray God's Will: Continuing the Journey.*
                 Philadelphia: The Westminster Press.
1987b   *To Will God's Will: Beginning the Journey.*
                 Philadelphia: The Westminster Press.
1988   *Pastoral Spirituality: A Focus for Ministry.*
                 Philadelphia, Pa.: The Westminster Press.
1990   *Discerning God's Will.* Louisville, Ky.:
                 Westminster/John Knox Press.
1998   "Forgiveness." *Journeyers:* A Newsletter of
                 Columbia Theological Seminary's Spirituality
                 Program, No 1.

Jones, L. Gregory
1995   *Embodying Forgiveness: A Theological Analysis.*
                 Grand Rapids, Mich.: William B. Eerdmans
                 Publishing Company.

Juel, Donald
1993   "The Lord's Prayer in the Gospels of Matthew
                 and Luke" in Daniel L. Migliore, ed. *The Lord's
                 Prayer: Perspectives for Reclaiming Christian
                 Prayer.* Grand Rapids, Mich.: William B.
                 Eerdmans Publishing Company.

Kelly, Geffrey B., ed.
1992   *Karl Rahner: Theologian of the Graced Search for
                 Meaning.* Minneapolis, Minn.: Fortress Press.

Law, William
1955   *A Serious Call to a Devout and Holy Life.*
                 Philadelphia, Pa.: The Westminster Press.

Lea, Larry
1995   *Could You Not Tarry One Hour?* Lake Mary,
                 Fla.: Creation House.

L'Engle, Madeleine
1980   *Walking on Water: Reflections on Faith and Art.*
                 Wheaton, Ill.: Harold Shaw Publishers.

Libby, Bob
1992   *The Forgiveness Book*. Boston, Mass.: Cowley
                Publications.

Lochman, Jan Milič
1993   "The Lord's Prayer in Our Time: Praying and
                Drumming" in Daniel L. Migliore, ed. *The Lord's
                Prayer: Perspectives for Reclaiming Christian
                Prayer*. Grand Rapids, Mich.: William B.
                Eerdmans Publishing Company.

Loder, James E.
1981   *The Transforming Moment: Understanding
                Convictional Experiences*. San Francisco: Harper
                & Row, Publishers.

Mays, James L.
1994   *The Lord Reigns: A Theological Handbook to the
                Psalms*. Louisville, Ky.: Westminster John Knox
                Press.

McDargh, John
1991   "The Drama That Is Prayer: A Psychoanalytic
                Interpretation" in William A. Barry and Kerry A.
                Maloney, eds. *A Hunger for God: Ten
                Approaches to Prayer*. Kansas City, Mo.: Sheed &
                Ward.

Meehan, Bridget
1990   *Nine Ways to Reach God*. Liguori, Mo.: Liguori
                Publications.

Merton, Thomas
1953   *Bread in the Wilderness*. Philadelphia, Pa.:
                Fortress Press.

Michael, Chester P. and Marie C. Norrisey
1984   *Prayer and Temperament: Different Prayer Forms
                for Different Personality Types*. Charlottesville,
                Va.: The Open Door.

Migliore, Daniel L., ed.
1993   "Preface" in *The Lord's Prayer: Perspectives
                for Reclaiming Christian Prayer*. Grand
                Rapids, Mich.: William B. Eerdmans Publishing
                Company.
1998   "Freedom to Pray: Karl Barth's Theology of
                Prayer" in Eric O. Springsted, ed., *Spirituality and
                Theology: Essays in Honor of Diogenes Allen*.
                Louisville, Ky.: Westminster John Knox Press.

Miller, Patrick D.
1994   *They Cried to the Lord: The Form and Theology
                of Biblical Prayer*. Minneapolis, Minn.: Fortress
                Press.

Morgenthaler, Sally
1998   " 'Out of the Box': Authentic Worship in a
                Postmodern Culture." *Worship Leader* (May-
                June).

Murray, Andrew
1982   *The Believer's School of Prayer*. Minneapolis,
                Minn.: Bethany House Publishers.

Peterson, Eugene
1989   *Answering God: The Psalms as Tools for Prayer*.
                San Francisco, Calif.: Harper & Row.

Purdy, John C.
1992   *Lord, Teach Us to Pray: Six Studies in Spirituality
                and the Lord's Prayer*. Pittsburgh, Pa.: The
                Kerygma Program.

Ramsey, Michael
1983   *Be Still and Know*. New York, N.Y.: The Seabury
                Press.

Sangster, W. E. and Leslie Davison
1962   *The Pattern of Prayer*. London: The Epworth
                Press.

Sardella, Dennis J.
1991　　　　　　　"Thoughts About Science and Prayer" in William
　　　　　　　　　A. Barry and Kerry A. Maloney, eds. *A Hunger*
　　　　　　　　　for God: Ten Approaches to Prayer. Kansas City,
　　　　　　　　　Mo.: Sheed & Ward.

Schleiermacher, Friedrich
1928　　　　　　　*The Christian Faith*. Edinburgh: T. & T. Clark.

Sheets, Dutch
1996　　　　　　　*Intercessory Prayer*. Ventura, Calif.: Regal Books.

Smith, Herbert, F.
1989　　　　　　　*Prayer and Personality Development*. Denville,
　　　　　　　　　N.J.: Dimension Books, Inc.

Spear, Wayne R.
1979　　　　　　　*The Theology of Prayer: A Systematic Study of*
　　　　　　　　　the Biblical Teaching on Prayer. Grand Rapids,
　　　　　　　　　Mich.: Baker Book House.

Stewart, George S.
1940　　　　　　　*The Lower Levels of Prayer*. New York, N.Y.:
　　　　　　　　　Abingdon-Cokesbury Press.

Teykl, Terry
1997　　　　　　　*Pray the Price*. Muncie, Ind.: Prayer Point Press.

Tillich, Paul
1951　　　　　　　*Systematic Theology Vol. I*. Chicago: The
　　　　　　　　　University of Chicago Press.
1963　　　　　　　*Systematic Theology Vol. III*. Chicago: The
　　　　　　　　　University of Chicago Press.

Torrey, R. A.
1900　　　　　　　*How to Pray*. New York, N.Y.: Fleming H. Revell
　　　　　　　　　Company.

Trueblood, Elton
1965   *The Lord's Prayers.* New York, N.Y.: Harper &
            Row, Publishers.

Williams, Charles
1942   *The Forgiveness of Sins.* Grand Rapids, Mich.:
            William B. Eerdmans Publishing Company.

Wink, Walter
1998   *The Powers That Be: Theology for a New
            Millennium.* New York, N.Y.: Doubleday.